CALIFORNIA EVIDENCE

L. LUBLINER

CALIFORNIA EVIDENCE

A Wizard's Guide

Gerald F. Uelmen
PROFESSOR OF LAW
SANTA CLARA UNIVERSITY
SCHOOL OF LAW

CAROLINA ACADEMIC PRESS
Durham, North Carolina

Copyright © 2005
Gerald F. Uelmen
All Rights Reserved

Library of Congress Cataloging-in-Publication Data

Uelmen, Gerald F.
California evidence : a wizard's guide / by Gerald F. Uelmen.
p. cm.
ISBN 1-59460-152-6 (alk. paper)
1. Evidence (Law)--California. I. Title.

KFC1030.Z9.U33 2005
347.794'06--dc22

2005017287

Carolina Academic Press
700 Kent Street
Durham, NC 27701
Telephone (919) 489-7486
Fax (919) 493-5668
www.cap-press.com

Printed in the United States of America.

*To the Memory of
Dr. Jean Uelmen
1947–2005*

Free at last!

Contents

Acknowledgments		xi
Introduction		xiii
What Is "Evidence"?		xv

Part I General Principles of Relevance

Chapter One	The Problem of Proposition Eight	3
Chapter Two	Probativeness and Materiality	7
Chapter Three	Conditional Relevance	11
Chapter Four	Probativeness vs. Prejudice	15

Part II Exclusion to Promote Extrinsic Policy

Introduction	Extrinsic to What?	23
Chapter Five	Jury Deliberations	25
Chapter Six	Subsequent Remedial Measures	27
Chapter Seven	Compromise Offers	29
Chapter Eight	Liability Insurance	31
Chapter Nine	Plea Bargaining in Criminal Cases	33

Part III Character Evidence

Introduction	A Road Map	37
Chapter Ten	The Character-Propensity Rule and Its Exceptions	41
Chapter Eleven	Propensity Evidence in Sexual Assault and Domestic Violence Cases	47
Chapter Twelve	Proof of Defendant's and Victim's Character	49
Chapter Thirteen	Rape Victims and the Rape Shield Law	51
Chapter Fourteen	Evidence of Habit	53
Chapter Fifteen	Character for Truthfulness	55
Chapter Sixteen	Review Materials for Character Evidence	61

Part IV Competency and Personal Knowledge

| Chapter Seventeen | Competency of Witnesses | 69 |
| Chapter Eighteen | Personal Knowledge | 73 |

Part V The Hearsay Rule and Its Exceptions

Chapter Nineteen	Hearsay Defined	79
Chapter Twenty	Party Admissions	81
Chapter Twenty-One	Prior Statements of a Witness	85
Chapter Twenty-Two	Past Recollection Recorded and Recollection Refreshed	89
Chapter Twenty-Three	Spontaneous and Contemporaneous Statements, and Statements of Physical or Mental Condition	91
Chapter Twenty-Four	Business and Official Records Exceptions	95
Chapter Twenty-Five	Unavailability Exceptions	97
Chapter Twenty-Six	Former Testimony	101
Chapter Twenty-Seven	The Constitutional Right of Confrontation and New Hearsay Exceptions	105
Chapter Twenty-Eight	Review of Hearsay Exceptions	109

Part VI Examining Witnesses

Chapter Twenty-Nine	Opinions and Experts	117
Chapter Thirty	Authentication	121
Chapter Thirty-One	The Best Evidence and Secondary Evidence Rules	123
Chapter Thirty-Two	Evidentiary Objections	125

Part VII Privileges

| Chapter Thirty-Three | Privileges in General | 133 |
| Chapter Thirty-Four | The Attorney-Client Privilege | 137 |

Part VIII Presumptions and Judicial Notice

| Chapter Thirty-Five | Presumptions | 143 |
| Chapter Thirty-Six | Judicial Notice | 147 |

CONTENTS

Practice Transcripts

A.	People v. Corleone (Murder Conspiracy)	151
B.	Pringle v. Dimwit Dodge, Inc. (Negligent Entrustment)	155
C.	People v. Rick E. Pugnant (Child Molestation)	159
D.	People v. Angela Muerta (Hospital Murders)	163
E.	People v. Don Defiler (Drug Possession)	167
F.	People v. Hart (Murder by Poison)	171
G.	People v. Dowling (Spousal Murder)	177
H.	Pringle v. Thomas & Neeley (Sexual Harassment)	183
J.	Price v. Ford Motor Co. (Wrongful Death)	189
K.	People v. Scott (Spousal Murder)	195
L.	People v. Defiler (Rape)	201

Objections to Transcripts

A.	People v. Corleone	209
B.	Pringle v. Dimwit Dodge	210
C.	People v. Pugnant	210
D.	People v. Angela Muerta	211
E.	People v. Don Defiler	212
F.	People v. Wilma Hart	213
G.	People v. Howard Dowling	214
H.	Paula Pringle v. Thomas & Neeley	215
J.	Pearl Price v. Ford Motor Co.	216
K.	People v. Peter Scott	218
L.	People v. Don Defiler	219

Epilogue	223
Index	225

Acknowledgments

Thank you to Dean Mack Player, Dean Don Polden and the Faculty of Santa Clara University School of Law, whose encouragement and support made this book possible. Thank you to Professor George Fisher of Stanford Law School, for reading the manuscript and offering many helpful suggestions. Thank you to Don Fiedler of Omaha, Nebraska, also known as Don Defiler, for his wizardry. Thank you to Chuck Sevilla of San Diego, California, for his ingenious "mantra motion." Thank you to Professors Ellen Kreitzberg, Bob Peterson, Kandis Scott and Chuck Gillingham, my fellow Evidence teachers at Santa Clara, for their insight and advice. Thank you to the students in my Evidence Courses for your many corrections and suggestions for improvement. And thank you to my wife, Martha Uelmen, for her inspiration.

Introduction

In reading the Harry Potter novels, I was struck by the many parallels between Hogwarts School of Wizardry and the typical American law school. The "sorting hat" that assigns students to the various Hogwarts dormitories bears a strong resemblance to the L.S.A.T. The curriculum for the budding wizards often looks like our law school curriculum. As an Evidence teacher, I sometimes imagine myself as a Hogwarts Professor teaching the course in "Magical Incantations." Many students enter the course in Evidence hoping it will teach them to be wizards in the courtroom, who can make evidence disappear by intoning the correct magical incantation. "Objection, this document is irrelevant and immaterial hearsay." "Sustained." It's just like waving a magic wand. The more profound message of Harry Potter, of course, is that there is "a lot more to magic...than waving your wand and saying a few funny words." [Rowling, *Harry Potter and the Sorcerer's Stone*, p.133]. Hogwarts' students get into the most trouble when they use their magical powers without sorting out all of its consequences. Likewise, a good lawyer doesn't make evidence appear or disappear without sorting out the ultimate impact upon the case to be proven or defeated. For the good lawyer, there are very few surprises in the courtroom. Nearly every evidentiary move has been anticipated and planned.

There is still another parallel between the neophyte wizards of Hogwarts and the student of Evidence. Often, the incantations pronounced by student wizards don't work, simply because they lack confidence that they *will* work. Confidence is a crucial ingredient for a successful trial lawyer, too. The confidence, however, comes from lots of patient practice.

In offering this text as a "Wizard's Guide," it comes with lots of opportunities for practice. The second half of the book is a series of fictional trial transcripts. They have been fully "tested," having been used as final examinations in a law school Evidence course. There are "answer guides" for each transcript in the Appendix, to take you to the objections that can be asserted. But one of the unique values of our "Wizard's Guide" is the references to the practice transcripts in the text itself. Follow the wand to the referenced transcript excerpts, and you will see an example of how the rule being discussed might be applied in a trial setting.

The Chapters in this Guide are broken up so that the applicable provisions of the California Evidence Code can be assigned at the same time that the corresponding rules of the Federal Rules of Evidence [FRE] are being covered in the typical law school casebook. It is assumed that you have a copy of the California Evidence Code [CEC]. Start each chapter by reading the language of the particular sections to be focused on. There are lots of differences between the Federal Rules and the California Evidence Code. This guide summarizes many of the differences in helpful charts. The transcripts all illustrate the application of the California Evidence Code. But always ask yourself whether the ruling would come out the same way in federal court.

What Is "Evidence"?

Focus on CEC 140, 190, 250, 353, 355, 400 and 401

1. California Evidence Code (CEC) 140 offers a useful definition of "evidence." It includes:
(a) "testimony," which comes in the form of answers to the questions posed to witnesses who appear in the courtroom;
(b) "writings," defined in CEC 250 to include any means of recording upon any tangible thing any form of communication or representation;
(c) "material objects," such as a weapon, a glove, a baggy of marijuana or a drop of blood; and
(d) "other things presented to the senses," such as the physical appearance of a person.
The definition, however, only includes those items which "are offered to prove the existence or non-existence of a fact." What if something the jurors can plainly observe is never formally "offered" as evidence? Assume, for example, the defendant is charged with a violation of California Penal Code §261.5, which provides:

> Any person 21 years of age or older who engages in an act of unlawful sexual intercourse with a minor who is under 16 years of age is guilty of [a crime].

The victim testifies that she was 15 when she engaged in an act of sexual intercourse with the defendant. In closing argument, the prosecutor points to the defendant sitting in the courtroom and argues, "You can see by looking at him that the defendant is over 21. He has grey hair, is balding, has wrinkles, and looks like he's at least forty years old." Is the defendant's physical appearance "evidence"? Was it formally "offered"? How would you go about "offering" it?

In *People v. Collie,* 110 Cal.App.3d 104, 167 Cal.Rptr. 720 (1980), the defendant wore dark glasses when he testified. In cross-examination of the defendant, the prosecutor asked why he was wearing dark glasses. The defendant responded that his eyes were sensitive to light and that he had always worn dark glasses for over twenty years, pursuant to a doctor's orders, except when he slept. The prosecutor then offered a photograph of the defendant in which he was not wearing dark glasses, and elicited testimony from one of the defendant's witnesses that he told her he wore dark glasses because "he liked them," and never mentioned any eye problems. In closing argument, the prosecutor argued to the jury as follows:

> When you talk to someone as I talk to you now, if I was wearing dark glasses would you wonder what my eyes were doing, would you wonder where I was looking, would you wonder what I was trying to hide? When I was cross-examining Mr. Collie I was thinking the same thing. Why? Because I couldn't see his eyes. So I was concerned about what kind of a reaction this jury is going to have to someone whose credibility they are asked to judge, when they can't even see what he looks like sitting on the stand answering questions, thinking about answers to questions.

The court concluded that the defendant's use of dark glasses was relevant evidence to assess his credibility, and the argument was not improper. Would the court's ruling be the same if the defendant had never been asked why he was wearing dark glasses? Is it improper for counsel to instruct a witness not to wear dark glasses? What if the lawyer suggests a witness get a shave or a haircut, or dress in a particular way to make a better impression on the jury?

2. If "evidence" can't be brought into the courtroom, the jury can be taken outside the courtroom to view it. A "jury view" is sometimes used to enable the jury to observe a crime scene, where the physical environment is an issue. In *People v. O.J. Simpson,* the jury was taken on a "jury view" to walk through the various rooms of Simpson's home. It was later claimed that defense attorney Johnny Cochran removed various photos of girlfriends from the walls, and replaced them with Norman Rockwell paintings, including the famous painting of a young black girl being escorted to a desegregated school by federal marshals. Is this any different than dressing up the defendant in a coat and tie when he's brought to court?

3. If "evidence" includes things "presented to the senses," should persons be included on juries who lack the senses to perceive the evidence? California Code of Civil Procedure §198, defining the competency of jurors, provides that "no person shall be deemed incompetent solely because of the loss of sight

or hearing in any degree or other disability which substantially impairs or interferes with the person's mobility."

4. What is the difference between "evidence" and "proof"? CEC 190 defines "proof" as "the establishment by evidence of a requisite degree of belief concerning a fact." The "elements" of a crime or a cause of action are facts which must be proved to the jury; the "evidence" is merely the *means* by which the facts are proved. But sometimes evidence cannot even be admitted until a factual prerequisite is established. For example, a confession is not admissible unless it is shown to be "voluntary." The factual prerequisite is called a "preliminary fact." CEC 400. If the admissibility of evidence depends upon a preliminary fact, the evidence is first "proffered." CEC 401. Only after the preliminary fact is "proven", in some cases to the judge, and in other cases to the jury, will the proffered evidence then be admissible.

5. An "objection" must be made to exclude inadmissible evidence. The California Evidence Code Sections relating to objections are summarized in Chapter 32, *infra*. If an appropriate objection is not made, it is ordinarily "waived," and the admission of the evidence cannot be challenged on appeal. FRE 103, CEC 353. An appropriate objection must be "timely made" and it must state specific legal grounds. A "motion to strike" will suffice if there was no opportunity to object in advance. CEC 353. A "motion in limine" can be used to raise an objection well in advance, outside the presence of the jury.

6. If an objection to a question is sustained, the witness will not be permitted to answer the question. However, counsel cannot argue on appeal that the erroneous sustaining of the objection was reversible error without showing it was prejudicial. The required showing of prejudice often requires an "offer of proof", in which the trial judge is informed of the substance, purpose and relevance of the anticipated answer. FRE 103(a)(2); CEC 354.

7. Frequently, evidence will be admitted to prove a particular fact, or against a particular party, but will *not* be admissible for a different purpose or against a different party. Under these circumstances, the jury must be instructed as to the restricted or limited use they are to make of the evidence. This is called a "limiting instruction." FRE 105, CEC 355.

Part I

General Principles of Relevance

CHAPTER ONE

THE PROBLEM OF PROPOSITION EIGHT

The California Evidence Code was drafted by the California Law Revision Commission, whose explanatory notes are a useful aid in interpreting the Code. The Code was approved by the California legislature with few changes, to take effect on January 1, 1967, eight years prior to the adoption of the Federal Rules of Evidence. Even though many states have since adopted the Federal Rules of Evidence to supply their state rules, California has not done so. The California Evidence Code thus applies in all court proceedings in California, with the exception of grand jury proceedings. [See Section 300, California Evidence Code]. While some sections of the Code specify that they only apply in criminal cases, and others only in civil cases, the same rules of evidence were generally intended to govern both civil and criminal cases in California. However, in June of 1982, the voters of California adopted Proposition 8, an initiative measure entitled "The Victims' Bill of Rights." This measure amended the California Constitution to prohibit the exclusion of relevant evidence in criminal proceedings. Article I, Section 28(d) of the California Constitution now provides:

> Except as provided by statute hereafter enacted by a two-thirds vote of the membership in each house of the Legislature, relevant evidence shall not be excluded in any criminal proceeding, including pretrial and post conviction motions and hearings, or in any trial or hearing of a juvenile for a criminal offense, whether heard in juvenile or adult court. Nothing in this section shall affect any existing statutory rule of evidence relating to privilege or hearsay, or Evidence Code Sections 352, 782 or 1103. Nothing in this section shall affect any existing statutory or constitutional right of the press.

Thus, with seven important exceptions, relevant evidence cannot be excluded in *criminal* cases in California, even though the same evidence *would* be excluded in civil cases. The seven exceptions are:

1. The *United States* constitution requires exclusion of the evidence. Although Section 28(d) of the California Constitution does not explicitly acknowledge it, the California Constitution cannot override the federal constitutional mandate in the Fourteenth Amendment of the U.S. Constitution providing that states cannot deprive any person of life, liberty or property without due process of law, or deny any person the equal protection of the laws. Thus, all of the "exclusionary rules" applied to the states through the due process clause by the U.S. Supreme Court apply in California, despite Proposition 8. For example, the requirement that evidence seized in violation of the Fourth Amendment prohibition of unreasonable searches and seizures be suppressed, *Mapp v. Ohio,* 367 U.S. 643 (1961); the rule that confessions obtained during custodial interrogation be suppressed unless the suspect voluntarily waives his Fifth Amendment privilege against self-incrimination, *Miranda v. Arizona,* 384 U.S. 436 (1966); and the rule that statements elicited from a suspect in violation of his Sixth Amendment right to counsel after criminal prosecution has been initiated be suppressed, *Massiah v. United States,* 377 U.S. 201 (1964), are all unaffected by Proposition 8. Proposition 8 does significantly limit California courts, however, by abrogating their power to create "exclusionary rules" for criminal cases based upon the state constitution.

2. Legislative enactments by a supermajority of two-thirds.
This is the most difficult exception to apply, since Code sections do not reveal the legislative margin by which they were enacted. Any new provisions added to the Evidence Code since Proposition 8 was enacted in 1982 which exclude relevant evidence will *not* apply to criminal proceedings unless they were enacted by a two-thirds vote. Happily, nearly all of the recently adopted or amended rules achieved the requisite two-thirds margin, including Section 351.1 (exclusion of polygraph examinations), Section 1101 (amended exclusion of evidence of character), and Section 1521 (Secondary Evidence Rule). Recently enacted new hearsay exceptions do not present a problem regarding the margin of enactment, since, of course, they do not *exclude* relevant evidence, but create an exception to allow its *admission.*

3. The rules of evidence relating to privilege.
Division 8 (Sections 900–1079) contains the sections of the California Evidence Code recognizing privileges, such as the Attorney-Client and Physician-Patient privileges. All of these privileges exclude relevant evidence, but are exempted from Proposition 8 by the language

of Section 28(d). Note, however, that the exemption only applies to "existing" rules of evidence relating to privilege. New statutory creations of privilege subsequent to Proposition 8 must meet the two-thirds supermajority requirement to apply in criminal cases. The privilege for mediation in Sections 1115–1128 of the California Evidence Code, adopted in 1997, does not apply to criminal cases because the legislature specified the privilege could only be invoked in "any arbitration, administrative adjudication, civil action, or other noncriminal proceeding." (Section 1119, California Evidence Code). Neither the Evidence Code nor Section 28(d) of Proposition 8 define the word "privilege". It can be argued that any rule which excludes evidence in order to protect the confidentiality of communications or preserve relationships defines a "privilege." There are statutory rules establishing such protection elsewhere than Division 8 of the Evidence Code. An important example is an offer to plead guilty (Section 1153).

4. The rules of evidence relating to hearsay.

The hearsay rule (Section 1200) excludes evidence which is relevant, but is exempted from Proposition 8 by the language of Section 28(d). *Exceptions* to the hearsay rule, of course, do not *exclude* evidence, but render it admissible. Thus, even hearsay exceptions enacted or amended since Proposition 8 (*e.g.,* Evidence Code Sections 1231, 1360, 1370 and 1380) will apply to criminal cases whether they were enacted by a two-thirds vote or not.

5. Evidence Code Section 352.

The discretion of a trial judge to exclude relevant evidence when its probative value is substantially outweighed by the dangers of prejudice, delay or confusion or misleading of the jurors remains unaffected by Proposition 8.

6. Evidence Code Sections 782 and 1103.

These sections, which contain California's "rape shield law" were exempted from Proposition 8 by the language of Section 28(d), although they clearly exclude relevant evidence.

7. Existing statutory or constitutional rights of the press.

This exemption is contained in Section 28(d) of Proposition 8, and was intended to insure that Proposition 8 could not be construed as an implied repeal of the broad protection for news reporters adopted two years before, as Proposition 5. Proposition 5 appears in Article I, Section 2(b) of the California Constitution, and prevents a court from holding a news reporter in contempt for refusing to disclose the identity of a source or any unpublished information obtained in gathering the news. This constitutional limitation will frequently result in the exclusion of relevant evidence.

Proposition 8 thus creates the "problem" that one cannot automatically assume that every section of the California Evidence Code has full application to civil and criminal cases. Like the Federal Rules of Evidence, some sections of the Evidence Code explicitly provide that they do not apply to criminal cases, and Proposition 8 is thus irrelevant. But even if a Code section explicitly applies to criminal cases, it may have been abrogated or limited by Proposition 8. If it operates to exclude relevant evidence, it cannot be applied in a criminal case unless it falls within one of the seven exceptions noted above.

Chapter Two

Probativeness and Materiality

Focus on CEC 210, 350 and 351

1. The Federal Rules of Evidence and the California Evidence Code define "relevant evidence" in essentially the same way. Both encompass the dual requirements of probativeness and materiality. Probative evidence has a tendency in reason to make a fact more or less likely than it would be without the evidence. [**Examples: F-48, G-8, J-99**]. Material evidence has a tendency to prove a fact of consequence to the action. [**Example: J-68**]. The Advisory Committee Note to FRE 401 acknowledges that some of its language was borrowed from CEC 210. But FRE 401 does *not* require that a fact be "in dispute" for the evidence proving it to be relevant. The Advisory Committee Note suggests that Rule 403 be used to exclude evidence offered to prove facts that are not in dispute, rather than a ruling that the evidence is irrelevant. CEC 210 defines relevant evidence to be evidence offered to prove or disprove "any disputed fact" that is of consequence. Also, CEC 210 clearly provides that evidence probative of the credibility of a witness or hearsay declarant is relevant evidence. Such evidence would be equally relevant under the FRE, as FRE 608 and 806 make clear. [**Examples: F-55, G-26**].
2. The legal standard of "relevancy" may have great significance in seeking pre-trial discovery. "An appellate court cannot reverse a trial court's grant of discovery under a 'relevancy' attack unless it concludes that the answers sought by a given line of questioning cannot as a reasonable possibility lead to the discovery of admissible evidence or be helpful in preparation for trial." *Pacific Tel.&Tel. Co. v. Superior Court,* 2 Cal.3d 161, 173 (1970).
   In *Morales v. Superior Court,* 99 Cal.App.3d 283 (1979), the plaintiff brought a tort claim for wrongful death of his wife against the trucking com-

pany whose negligence allegedly caused her death. His three children also sought damages for the loss of their mother. The defendant trucking company served an interrogatory upon the plaintiff, demanding that he:

> State the name, current address and telephone number of each woman he dated during his marriage to Phyllis Morales and the calendar dates upon which he saw these women socially,...and whether during the period of his marriage to Phyllis Morales [he] had sexual relations with women other than Phyllis Morales, and if so,...state the names, current addresses and telephone numbers of each woman with whom he had sexual relations during that time and the date or dates of the sexual relations with each woman so identified.

Why might this interrogatory lead to the discovery of admissible relevant evidence?

In ruling that the interrogatory had to be answered, the Court noted it was not a "fishing expedition." The plaintiff remarried after his wife's death, and then divorced his second wife, who stated in a deposition that plaintiff dated and "possibly had frequent sexual relations" with other women during his marriage to Phyllis.

The Court did find that any women he dated were protected by a right of privacy that was not forfeited by his filing of a lawsuit. Therefore, the requirement that he provide the names, addresses and telephone numbers of his companions was struck, but the plaintiff was required to state whether, "during some relevant period," he dated other women and whether he had "extramarital contacts." What period of time would be "relevant" if the plaintiff had been married to Phyllis for 25 years?

What if the plaintiff is seeking damages for sexual harassment? Could an interrogatory seeking information about prior sexual activity of the defendant lead to the discovery of admissible relevant evidence? See Cal. Code of Civil Procedure §2017(d), and *Knoettgen v. Superior Court*, 224 Cal.App.3d 11 (1990).

Would evidence that the defendant "dated" other women be relevant in a criminal prosecution for the murder of his wife? Could it establish a motive for the murder? [**Examples: K-37, K-115**].

3. There is an important difference between civil and criminal cases in the ability of the parties to directly control what are "disputed facts...of consequence to the determination of the action." In a criminal prosecution, the accused only has two choices: a plea of "guilty," admitting all of the allegations in the charge, or a plea of "not guilty," putting all allegations at issue. Absent a stipulation, the prosecution can rightly insist that evidence be admitted to

prove *every* element beyond a reasonable doubt. In a civil case, however, the defendant can admit some of the allegations in the complaint, eliminating them as issues from the trial. In *Fuentes v. Tucker*, 31 Cal.2d 1 (1947), for example, the defendant filed an amended answer admitting liability for the wrongful deaths of children who were killed when he struck them with his car. The case then proceeded to trial on the issue of damages. Over defendant's objection, the trial court admitted evidence that the defendant was intoxicated and that the children were thrown eighty feet by the impact. The California Supreme Court held that it was error to admit the evidence, since it was no longer material.

4. The U.S. Supreme Court in *Old Chief v. United States*, 519 U.S. 172 (1997), held that a federal trial judge must accept a stipulation that a defendant charged with possession of a firearm by a convicted felon is a convicted felon, and that it was error for the lower court to allow the prosecutor to prove the nature of the felony conviction. Note that the *Old Chief* case is *not* a constitutional ruling; it construes the FRE, and would only be controlling in a federal prosecution.

Would a California defendant who offered to stipulate to the fact of a prior conviction get the same result under the CEC? In *People v. Hall*, 28 Cal.3d 143 (1980), the California Supreme Court construed the CEC in the same way the U.S. Supreme Court construed the FRE, and held that the defendant's offer to stipulate must be accepted over the prosecutor's objection. Two years later, however, partly in response to the *Hall* opinion, the prosecutors who drafted Proposition 8 inserted a constitutional amendment which provides:

> Any prior felony conviction of any person in any criminal proceeding, whether adult or juvenile, shall subsequently be used without limitation for purposes of impeachment or enhancement of sentence in any criminal proceeding. *When a prior felony conviction is an element of any felony offense, it shall be proven to the trier of fact in open court.*

Calif. Const., Art. I, §28(f) (emphasis supplied). In *People v. Valentine*, 42 Cal.3d 170 (1986), the defendant was accused of being an ex-felon in possession of a concealable firearm. To prevent the jury from learning the nature of his prior offenses, he offered to stipulate that he had prior felony convictions. Relying on Proposition 8, the trial judge rejected the stipulation, and held that the prosecution was entitled to prove the prior convictions by offering the judgments in evidence. The California Supreme Court reversed, holding that the language of Proposition 8 limits the prosecution to proof of the fact of conviction, not its nature. Proposition 8 "does not require the nature of prior convictions to go to the jury in such a case, since that information is utterly irrelevant to the charge." *Id.* at 181–82. What if the language of Proposition 8 were changed, to read, "When a prior conviction is an element of any felony offense, both the fact of conviction and its nature shall be proven to the trier of fact in open court." Would such a provision violate the United States Constitution? Is there any constitutional right for a criminal defendant to have his guilt determined only on the basis of relevant evidence?

In *Spencer v. Texas,* 385 U.S. 554, 567–68 (1967), the Supreme Court upheld a procedure in which the jury decided the sentence at the same time it decided guilt, even though some of the evidence before it was relevant only to the sentence, noting that the jury was instructed not to consider the sentencing evidence when determining guilt. *Accord, McGautha v. California,* 402 U.S. 183, 209 (1971). In *People v. Castro,* 38 Cal.3d 301, 314 (1985), however, the California Supreme Court held that the admission of irrelevant evidence on the issue of guilt or innocence would violate the defendant's constitutional right to due process of law.

Chapter Three

Conditional Relevance

Focus on CEC 400–405

1. There is a fundamental difference between the Federal Rules of Evidence and the California Evidence Code with respect to the proof of preliminary facts that determine the admissibility of evidence. Under FRE 104(a), when a preliminary fact is determined by the *judge*, the judge is "not bound by the rules of evidence except those with respect to privilege."[1] This means that a judge can consider inadmissible hearsay in making the preliminary ruling, and even rely upon the proffered evidence itself before its admission to determine whether it is admissible. This is appropriately called "boot-strapping," an allusion to pulling oneself up by one's own bootstraps. [Try it! You won't get off the ground!] Where the preliminary fact is determined by the jury, or finder of fact, however, FRE 104(b) requires admissible evidence to be introduced, "sufficient to support a finding of the condition."

The California Evidence Code does not permit "boot-strapping." Regardless of who decides the preliminary issue, it must be proved by admissible evidence. As noted in the Advisory Committee Note to FRE 104, the drafters of the California Evidence Code explicitly rejected a proposal similar to FRE 104(a). The California parallel to FRE 104(a) is CEC 405.

2. Whether a preliminary fact is decided by judge or jury under the California Evidence Code is determined by whether the relevance of the evidence depends upon the existence of the disputed preliminary fact, just as under the Federal Rules of Evidence. Issues of "conditional relevance" are determined by

---

1. There actually are no "Rules of Evidence" with respect to privilege in the FRE, because they were deleted by Congress when the FRE was enacted. Rule 501 declares that privileges shall be governed by the principles of common law. Presumably, Rule 104(a) would require a judge to apply the common law of privilege in determining preliminary questions.

the jury under both the FRE and the CEC, but some issues that are treated as questions of conditional relevance under the CEC are not considered questions of conditional relevance under the FRE.

CEC 403 is the California equivalent of FRE 104(b), but it is much more detailed. Does it need to be? Section 403(a) defines four categories of preliminary questions to be determined by the trier of fact upon submission of evidence "sufficient to support a finding:"

1. The relevance of the proffered evidence depends upon the existence of the preliminary fact;
2. The preliminary fact is the personal knowledge of a witness concerning the subject matter of his testimony;
3. The preliminary fact is the authenticity of a writing; or
4. The proffered evidence is of a statement or other conduct of a particular person and the preliminary fact is whether that person made the statement or so conducted himself.

Are not (2), (3) and (4) simply additional examples of (1)? Under the FRE, the personal knowledge of a witness must also be first established by "evidence sufficient to support a finding" [See FRE 602]; the authenticity of a writing must also be first established by evidence "sufficient to support a finding" [See FRE 901(a)]; and the identity of the person who made a statement or engaged in particular conduct will also be first established by evidence "sufficient to support a finding" [See Comment to FRE 104(b)]. The reason, of course, is that these are *all* examples of conditional relevance.

3. The FRE and the CEC part company on the question of "conditional relevance" with respect to the preliminary determinations that (1) a party authorized another person to make a particular statement, (2) a particular statement was within the scope of an agent or servant's employment, and (3) a particular statement was in furtherance of a conspiracy of which both the speaker and the person against whom the statement is offered were members. These preliminary facts must be established to bring a statement within the hearsay exceptions for party admissions. When we get to the hearsay rule and study these exceptions, we will see that under FRE 104(a) all of these issues are decided by the judge, even though they are clearly issues of conditional relevance. There does not seem to be any logical explanation for this aberration, other than a fundamental misunderstanding of the meaning of conditional relevance, which was subsequently incorporated as an amendment to the FRE. Under the CEC, each of these facts is treated as a question of conditional relevance, to be determined by the finder of fact under CEC 403 upon the submission of evidence sufficient to support a finding. [See CEC 1222, 1223].

Note that the difference between the FRE and the CEC on this point not only affects who determines the preliminary factual issue, but also whether "boot-strapping" will be permitted in making the determination. Under the FRE, "boot-strapping" is only permitted in making FRE 104(a) determinations. In moving the preliminary factual determinations for these three hearsay exceptions from FRE 104(b) to FRE 104(a), the Federal Rules permit the factual determinations to be based on "boot-strapping," which is not permitted under the CEC, and would not be permitted under FRE 104(b).

4. Study the Comments of the Assembly Committee on the Judiciary to CEC 403 and 405 very carefully. They offer a very useful catalog of examples of the kind of preliminary questions that would be decided as questions of conditional relevance under CEC 403, and those that would be decided by the judge under CEC 405. Throughout the course, as you encounter preliminary "foundation" facts that are prerequisites to the admissibility of evidence, ask yourself whether these facts would be determined by the finder of fact as a CEC 403/FRE 104(b) question, or by the judge as a CEC 405/FRE 104(a) question.

5. Under CEC 403(b), the judge has discretion to admit evidence conditionally, even if evidence sufficient to support a finding of the preliminary fact has not yet been offered, subject to the necessary evidence being offered later in the trial. If it is not later offered, the evidence is subject to a Motion to Strike, and may even require a mistrial if the jury cannot be reasonably expected to put it aside. There are two important exceptions, where the judge does not have discretion: a party can insist that evidence of personal knowledge of a witness be established before the witness is permitted to testify, and a party can insist that an expert's qualifications be elicited before he gives an opinion. There is no similar protection under the Federal Rules of Evidence; the judge always has discretion to control the order of presenting evidence. [FRE 611(a)].

6. Note that CEC 403(c) provides that the court "may, and on request shall, instruct the jury to determine whether the preliminary fact exists and to disregard the proffered evidence unless the jury finds that the preliminary fact does exist."

In the O.J. Simpson murder trial, the prosecution offered evidence that a sample of blood found on the back gate of Nicole Brown's apartment three weeks after the murder was "matched" with O.J. Simpson's blood through D.N.A. analysis. The defense contended that the blood was "planted" on the back gate after the murder occurred and presented evidence that the sample contained EDTA, a preservative used to prevent the coagulation of blood samples in test tubes, but which is not naturally present in human blood. Is the question of whether the blood sample was "planted" an issue of conditional relevance to be decided by the jury? Should the jury have been instructed to disregard the evidence of the D.N.A. match unless they first found that the blood sample was deposited on the gate at the time of the murder? How would you instruct the jury?

The defense submitted the following request for a special jury instruction to Judge Ito, citing CEC 403(c) as authority:

> Evidence of the comparison of blood which was not discovered on the back gate at the Bundy crime scene until July 3, 1994...with a blood sample provided by Mr. Simpson...has been introduced for the purpose of showing the identity of the perpetrator of the murders. Before you may even consider such evidence, you must first determine whether the blood found on the back gate...was deposited by the perpetrator...of the murders on June 12, 1994. If you find that the blood may have been deposited on the back gate...at some time subsequent to June 12, 1994, however, you must disregard this evidence and not consider it for any purpose.

Judge Ito rejected the request, and instead instructed the jury as follows:

> The court has admitted physical evidence such as blood, hair and fiber evidence, and experts' opinions concerning the analysis of such physical evidence. You are the sole judges of whether any such evidence has a tendency in reason to prove any fact at issue in this case. You should carefully review and consider all of the circumstances surrounding each item of evidence, including but not limited to its discovery, collection, storage and analysis. If you determine that any item of evidence does not have a tendency in reason to prove any element of the crimes charged or the identity of the perpetrator of the crimes charged, you must disregard such evidence.

Did Judge Ito's instruction comply with CEC 403(c)? If the jury concluded that blood evidence had actually been "planted", could it then infer that *other* evidence produced by officers of the Los Angeles Police Department should be distrusted? If so, did the defense really want the jury to be instructed that if blood were deposited on the back gate some time subsequent to June 12, the evidence may not be considered *for any purpose?*

Chapter Four

Probativeness vs. Prejudice

Focus on CEC 352

1. FRE 403 and CEC 352 both give the judge discretion to exclude relevant evidence, both require that "probative value" be "substantially outweighed," and both list the "dangers" of prejudicing, confusing or misleading the jury. FRE 403 also permits "considerations of undue delay, waste of time, or needless presentation of cumulative evidence," while CEC 352 simply speaks of necessitating "undue consumption of time." Can you think of circumstances where an "undue delay" or the presentation of cumulative evidence would *not* necessitate "undue consumption of time"?

Also note that "substantial" appears twice in CEC 352, requiring that probative value be *substantially* outweighed by *substantial* danger of undue prejudice, or confusing the issues, or misleading the jury. Does this require a greater showing of danger of prejudice, confusion or misleading than FRE 403? [**Examples: E-20, E-22, F-32**].

2. When a FRE 403 or CEC 352 objection is made to grisly crime scene or autopsy photos, ordinarily the judge simply examines the proffered photos to determine if the danger of prejudice substantially outweighs their probative value. In the case of *People v. O.J. Simpson,* the defense asked the judge to examine all of the autopsy photos available, including ones the prosecution had not proffered, arguing:

> The availability of alternative photographs which may be less prejudicial than those selected by the People would establish that there is no compelling evidentiary need to subject jurors to highly inflammatory photographs that may have been selected for their shock value rather than for legitimate evidentiary purposes.

Do FRE 403 or CEC 352 *require* the judge to consider whether less prejudicial alternatives are available to the prosecutor to prove the same facts as the proffered evidence? Do they *permit* the judge to do so?

3. Both FRE 403 and CEC 352 refer to prejudicing, confusing or misleading *the* jury, not *a* jury. Does this mean the judge should assess the impact that the evidence is likely to have upon the jurors actually sitting to try the case, or upon a hypothetical objective "reasonable jury"? In the trial of *People v. O.J. Simpson*, the prosecution argued in a CEC 352 objection to the judge that evidence of the use of the inflammatory racial epithet "nigger" by Detective Fuhrman would be particularly prejudicial in its effect upon the black persons actually sitting on the jury:

> But Mr. Cochran and the defense, they have a purpose in going into that area and that purpose is to inflame the passions of the jury and to ask them to pick sides not on the basis of the evidence in this case. And the evidence in this case against this defendant is overwhelming. There is a mountain of evidence pointing to this defendant's guilt. But when you mention that word to this jury or to any African American, it blinds people. It will blind the jury, it will blind them to the truth. They won't be able to discern what is true and what is not. It will affect their judgment, it will impair their ability to be fair and impartial. It will cause extreme prejudice to the prosecution's case.... Another thing hearing that word causes black people to do,... it causes you to change your focus. It diverts your attention. If we really want the jury's attention focused on the evidence and on the legal and factual issues... we shouldn't let them hear this word, because if they hear this word they are going to focus their attention on the issue of race. They are going to be more concerned with whether Mark Fuhrman is a racist than they are with whether there wasn't any way, and possibility, and chance, any theory offered by the defense to establish that Mark Fuhrman planted evidence. That will be a foregone conclusion. They can just check that one off. He must have done it, he is a racist. That is what Mr. Cochran wants the jury to do, skip the evidence, forget the direct examination and the cross examination and the real factual points established in the case. The jury is going to find this case on the basis of race. They are all going to be preoccupied with race. After all, Mr. Simpson is an African American, and so is Mr. Cochran.

Defense Lawyer Johnny Cochran responded:

It is demeaning to our jurors to say that African Americans who have lived under oppression for 200 plus years in this country cannot work within the mainstream, cannot hear these offensive words. African Americans live with offensive words, offensive looks, offensive treatment every day of their lives, but yet they still believe in this country. And to say that our jurors, because they hear this offensive word—to say they can't be fair is absolutely outrageous.... To try and pretend that racism doesn't exist in this country is to bury one's head in the sand. It is the height of naivete. Nobody wants to introduce race into this case, Your Honor, but as Mr. Darden has pointed out, race plays a part of everything in America.

Judge Ito ruled as follows:

The prosecution's last request is for an order by this court to prohibit the use in this case of the "N-word." The prosecution made an impassioned and heartfelt plea for this court to contemplate and understand the vile, repulsive and explosive nature of that epithet. The prosecution strongly argues that this epithet is so vile that it operates as a divisive demand that those to whom it is said take some action, and that its use can cloud the operation of good judgment and common sense. Defense counsel, in equally impassioned and heartfelt tones, argues that it gives little credit to jurors in general and African Americans serving as jurors in particular to assert that they will be so inflamed by the use of this epithet that they will ignore their oaths as trial jurors to determine this case based upon the evidence presented and the law as instructed. Both arguments have merit. The racial divisions that exist in this country remain the last great challenge to us as a Nation. How we evolve and hopefully solve the problem will be our memorial in history. When meritorious arguments are raised on both sides, the court must always remember this process is a search for the truth and that it depends upon the sound judgment of our jurors. If the challenged racial epithet was used in a relevant incident, it will be heard in court.

Is it appropriate to address the question of prejudicing the jury in terms of the particular composition of the jury selected to hear the case? Should judges make different rulings on the admissibility of evidence depending upon the racial composition of the jury? Their educational backgrounds or gender?
4. The concept of undue or unfair "prejudice" does not mean that the evidence will have overwhelming persuasive power; it usually means that there is a risk the evidence will be used to draw improper or inappropriate inferences other

than those the evidence was offered to establish. For example, evidence that the defendant previously committed the same crime he is now charged with may be relevant and admissible to show that he committed the charged crime with the requisite intent or knowledge, but it might also give rise to an inference of propensity, *i.e.*, he did it once, so it's more likely he did it again. From this perspective, while circumstantial evidence is frequently excluded under Section 352, direct evidence is rarely excluded because of the danger of unfair or undue prejudice. On the other hand, direct evidence may be excluded because it is cumulative or requires undue consumption of time. If thirty eyewitnesses all saw the same thing at the same time, would any court permit a party to call all thirty of them? Why not? [**Examples: B-55, B-60**].

5. Frequently the response to an objection under FRE 403 or CEC 352 is that the Court can prevent the potential prejudice by giving the jury a limiting instruction, reminding them to consider the evidence only for the limited purpose for which it was admitted. If evidence is admitted for a limited purpose, FRE 105 and CEC 355 both require the court to give a limiting instruction upon request. Failure to make the request, however, will constitute a waiver of the issue on appeal.

6. Section 352 of the California Evidence Code is one of the explicit exceptions to Proposition 8, permitting the exclusion of relevant evidence in criminal cases. If the "all relevant evidence" provision of Proposition 8, Calif. Const. Art. I, Section 28(d) abrogates a statutory rule of exclusion based on extrinsic policy, could the trial judge achieve the same result by utilizing Section 352? Consider, for example, the exclusion of an offer to plead guilty in CEC 1153. This section was enacted to promote the public policy of encouraging plea bargaining. Since it excludes relevant evidence (an admission of guilt) and since it does not fall within any Proposition 8 exception, CEC 1153 no longer applies in criminal cases. If a defendant's offer to plead guilty in exchange for a reduced sentence is rejected, and the prosecutor then presents the offer to plead guilty as evidence, could the judge exclude it under Section 352? Can the frustration of public policy ever supply undue or unfair prejudice? Despite the demise of CEC 1153, there is no recorded example of a California prosecutor ever using an offer to plead guilty during plea bargaining as evidence against the defendant. Why not?

7. Evidence of statistical probability might be excluded on the grounds it would mislead or confuse the jury. In *People v. Collins*, 68 Cal.2d 319, 66 Cal.Rptr. 497 (1968), for example, the prosecutor used the product rule of probability to multiply the factual variables in an identification, to suggest that the probability that the police apprehended the wrong suspects was one chance in 12 million. The California Supreme Court ruled the evidence should have

been excluded because of the risk that it would confuse the jury and distract them from focusing on the requirement of proof beyond a reasonable doubt. But in cases in which DNA evidence is admitted, California courts routinely permit evidence of the statistical probability that someone other than the defendant was the source of the blood or semen which was analyzed. [**Example: C-56**].

Part II

Exclusion to Promote Extrinsic Policy

Introduction

Extrinsic to What?

The sections of the California Evidence Code in this Part all appear in Division 9 of the Code, entitled "Evidence Affected or Excluded by Extrinsic Policies." By "extrinsic," we mean policies not related to the resolution of disputes in court, but to promote or encourage behavior in the "real world" outside of the courtroom. With respect to each of these rules, it is important to identify the extrinsic policy being promoted. The rules assume that behavior can be affected by how the rules of evidence treat that behavior; that manufacturers, for example, would not improve their products to make them safer if the remedial measure could be used against them in court as an admission that their product *needed* improvement, or that lawyers would not plea bargain and settle cases without trial if their offer to plead guilty could be offered against their clients as admissions. From this perspective, constitutional exclusionary rules are also based upon "extrinsic policy." Evidence from unlawful searches is excluded not because it is unreliable, but in order to discourage or "deter" police from violating the constitution, because they will have nothing to gain. With respect to constitutional exclusionary rules, however, like the *Miranda* decision, the "deterrent effect" of the evidentiary rule upon the behavior of police officers is hotly contested. Why wouldn't police officers be deterred by evidentiary exclusionary rules to the same extent as General Motors or criminal defense lawyers? It may be that gaining admissible evidence is not the primary motivation for many police investigative practices. To the same extent, we should question whether evidentiary rules promoting extrinsic policy are based upon a realistic assessment of what motivates behavior in the "real world."

These rules all exclude relevant evidence. What could be more relevant than an admission your product needs improvement, or an offer to plead guilty to the crime you are charged with in exchange for a lesser sentence? Thus, unless they can be characterized as rules relating to "privileges," they are *all* abrogated in criminal cases by Proposition 8. Most of them, however, have no application in criminal cases anyway. Only CEC 1150 and 1153 are actually affected by Section 28(d) of Proposition 8.

CHAPTER FIVE

JURY DELIBERATIONS

Focus on CEC 1150

1. There is a fundamental difference between CEC 1150, which *allows* evidence of statements or conduct in the jury room, but excludes evidence of the *effects* of such statements or conduct upon a juror's mental processes, and FRE 606(b), which excludes a juror's testimony as to "any matter or statement" during jury deliberations *as well as* the effect of "anything" upon a juror's mental processes. As the case of *Tanner v. United States,* 483 U.S. 107 (1987), illustrates, even evidence that jurors ingested drugs while deliberating was excluded when it came from one of the jurors. Such evidence would not be excluded under the California rule. Long before the California Evidence Code was adopted, the California Supreme Court was presented with an appeal by a defendant convicted of murder who complained that the jury deliberating his fate had consumed twenty gallons of beer, two casks of wine, and two bottles of whiskey, as well as other wine and whiskey at each meal, including breakfast. The conviction was reversed and the case was remanded for a new trial in a drier location. *People v. Gray,* 61 Cal. 164 (1882).

2. Recent statutory enactments and judicial decisions to protect juror privacy have made it difficult for California lawyers or their investigators to interview jurors and discover potential claims of juror misconduct. Calif. Code of Civil Procedure §237(a)(2) requires sealing of the personal identifying information of the jury upon the recording of a verdict. While lawyers can petition the court for access to personal jury information to communicate with jurors, such petitions must show "good cause," and can be objected to by any juror. Even if counsel has independent means available to identify and locate jurors, the California Supreme Court in *Townsel v. Superior Court,* 20 Cal.4th 1084 (1999) upheld the discretion of trial courts to forbid *any* contact of discharged jurors without obtaining the court's approval. *See* Uelmen, "Going Easy on

Juror Misconduct," California Lawyer Magazine, March, 2000, p. 30. In most California courtrooms today, jurors are identified only by number, and lawyers never even learn their names. The anonymity of jurors has been criticized as presenting substantial risks to the traditional deliberative process. Research of social psychologists suggests these risks could include undermining the presumption of innocence and diluting the standard of proof required for conviction. *See* Margolin & Uelmen, "The Anonymous Jury," ABA *Criminal Justice,* Fall, 1994, p. 14.

If anonymity is beneficial for jurors, why should the benefits of anonymity be *limited* to jurors? Why shouldn't everyone in the system be anonymous? A trial transcript might read:

> "Judge B-36: All right, call the case of People v. 8633972. Will counsel announce their appearances?
> Defense Counsel: State Bar No. 46096 appearing on behalf of defendant 8633972.
> Prosecutor: State Bar No. 67239 for the People.
> Judge B-36: All right, call your first witness.
> Prosecutor: The People call Witness No. C34P505."

What's wrong with this scenario? *Compare* Franz Kafka, *The Trial.*

3. Section 28(d) of Proposition 8 clearly applies to "post conviction motions and hearings." If an attorney, challenging a jury verdict in a criminal case, offers the testimony of a juror that, but for extraneous information supplied by another juror, he would not have voted to convict, is this relevant evidence? If so, does not Proposition 8 abrogate CEC 1150, and require the admission of the evidence?

Chapter Six

Subsequent Remedial Measures

Focus on CEC 1151

1. CEC 1151 excludes evidence of "remedial or precautionary measures" taken after an event which might have prevented an injury, when offered to "show negligence or culpable conduct. [**Example: B-43**]. In *Ault v. International Harvester*, 13 Cal.3d 113 (1974), the plaintiff was seriously injured when his "Scout" vehicle veered off an embankment. He brought an action alleging the accident was caused by a defect in the design of the vehicle, and sought recovery under theories of strict liability, breach of warranty, and negligence. The gear box of the Scout was made of aluminum 380, which the plaintiff contended was defective for that purpose. At trial, he offered evidence that after the accident, the defendant changed the gear boxes on Scout vehicles, making them of malleable iron. The trial judge admitted the evidence over an objection that its admission violated CEC 1151. The California Supreme Court, in an opinion by Justice Stanley Mosk, ruled that CEC 1151 has no application to a cause of action based upon strict liability, since strict liability does not encompass "culpable conduct." The Court found that the extrinsic policy which underlies CEC 1151 had no application to products liability cases:

> When the context is transformed from a typical negligence setting to the modern products liability field, however, the "public policy" assumptions justifying this evidentiary rule are no longer valid. The contemporary corporate mass producer of goods, the normal products liability defendant, manufactures tens of thousands of units of goods; it is manifestly unrealistic to suggest that such a producer will forego making improvements in its product, and risk innumerable additional lawsuits and the attendant adverse effect upon its public

image, simply because evidence of adoption of such improvement may be admitted in an action founded on strict liability for recovery on an injury that preceded the improvement.

13 Cal.3d at 120. [**Example: J-66**].

2. FRE 407 explicitly rejects the California exception recognized in *Ault*. But what if a California case were filed in federal court on the basis of diversity of citizenship? Would the federal court be required to apply the California rule, and admit evidence of subsequent remedial measures to show strict liability, by virtue of *Erie Railroad v. Thompkins*, 304 U.S. 64 (1938)? Does the exception recognized in *Ault* have a substantive purpose? Don't all the rules which exclude evidence to promote extrinsic policy have a "substantive purpose"? Federal courts have split on the question whether a federal court must follow the state rule in circumstances such as these. *Compare Flaminio v. Honda Motor Co.*, 733 F.2d 463, 470–73 (7th Cir. 1984) (Applying federal rule) *with Moe v. Avions Marcel Dassault-Breguet Aviation*, 727 F.2d 917, 932 (10th Cir. 1984) (Applying state rule).

3. FRE 407 now makes it clear that remedial measures taken after the original manufacture of a product, but before the injury giving rise to the lawsuit, *are* admissible, even to prove negligence. CEC 1151 still refers to remedial measures taken "after the occurrence of an event." If the "event" is the injury giving rise to the lawsuit, wouldn't we get the same result in California? *See Chase v. GMC*, 856 F.2d 17, 21–22 (4th Cir. 1988) (Construing FRE 407 prior to amendment to permit evidence of post-manufacture pre-injury remedial measures).

4. The defendant in *Ault* also complained that the trial court admitted evidence regarding two other accidents involving Scout vehicles, in which gear boxes made of aluminum 380 had allegedly failed. The California Supreme Court held that sufficient similarity between the accidents was shown to justify admission. Why would the other accidents be relevant to a cause of action based upon strict liability for a defective product? Why would they be relevant to a cause of action based upon negligence? Evidence of other accidents is admissible to prove a defective condition, knowledge, or the cause of an accident, provided that the circumstances of the other accidents are similar and not too remote. *Kopfinger v. Grand Central Pub. Market*, 60 Cal.2d 852 (1964). [**Examples: F-59, F-63, J-64**]. A similar test is applied to experiments to recreate the conditions that caused an event. [**Example: K-75**].

Chapter Seven

Compromise Offers

Focus on CEC 1152, 1154

1. FRE 408 includes both compromises of claims of liability, as well as claims which are disputed as to amount. The California Evidence Code treats the former in CEC 1152, and the latter in CEC 1154.
2. FRE 408 explicitly recognizes that exclusion is not required if the compromise is offered for a purpose *other than* proving liability or validity of a claim or its amount, such as proving bias or negativing undue delay. Would the evidence be admissible for such other purposes under CEC 1152 and 1154? [Example: H-82].
3. The legislative conference report for FRE 408 explains that the third sentence, which states "[t]his rule does not require the exclusion of any evidence otherwise discoverable merely because it is presented in the course of compromise negotiations," was added to meet the objection that a party could present a fact during compromise negotiations and thereby prevent an opposing party from offering evidence of that fact at trial, even though such evidence was obtained from independent sources. Could that happen under CEC 1152 or 1154, which do not have language like the third sentence of FRE 408?
4. Would FRE 408 protect statements made in the course of mediation of a disputed claim? Federal courts now mandate mediation, in conformity with the Alternative Dispute Resolution Act (the "ADRA"), enacted in 1998. Section 652(d) of the ADRA states that "each district court shall, by local rule... provide for the confidentiality of the alternative dispute resolution processes and...prohibit disclosure of confidential dispute resolution processes." The California Evidence Code also includes protection for communications during mediation. CEC 1119. The protection does not extend to subsequent criminal actions, however. The California Evidence Code also provides that a mediator shall not be competent to testify in a subsequent civil proceeding with respect to statements or conduct occurring during mediation. CEC 703.5.

In *Olam v. Congress Mortgage Co.,* 68 F.Supp.2d 1110 (1999), the court held that the ADRA provisions for confidentiality only apply to cases arising under federal law, and FRE 501 required application of the California rules with respect to confidentiality of mediation in a claim arising under state law. Then the court applied California law and ruled that CEC 703.5 is not an absolute preclusion of mediator testimony, since it is phrased in terms of *competency* rather than *privilege*. Since both the plaintiff and the defendant waived their confidentiality protection and wanted the court to consider evidence about what happened during the mediation, the court ruled that the mediator could not refuse to testify.

In *Foxgate Homeowner's Assoc. v. Bramalea California, Inc.,* 26 Cal. 4th 1 (2001), the California Supreme Court rejected a judicially crafted exception to mediation confidentiality which would have permitted mediators to report sanctionable conduct. The Court held the statutory confidentiality provisions were absolute, permitting no exceptions. *Olam* was found distinguishable, since the parties had waived confidentiality protection. 26 Cal. 4th at 17.

5. Would the provisions of CEC 1152 or 1154 protect statements made in negotiation of a civil claim from being admitted in a subsequent criminal trial? In *People v. Muniz,* 213 Cal.App.3d 1508 (1989), the prosecution offered evidence that the defendant, an alleged sex offender, had offered to pay for the victim's medical expenses. The court upheld the admission of the evidence, holding that CEC 1152 only applies when the evidence is offered to prove "liability," and this only includes *civil* liability. Even if CEC 1152 were construed to extend to criminal liability, wouldn't Proposition 8 prevent its application to criminal cases, because it excludes relevant evidence? [**Example: L-10**].

Chapter Eight

Liability Insurance

Focus on CEC 1155

1. FRE 411 extends to evidence that a person was *or was not* insured, while CEC 1155 only includes evidence that a person *was* insured. Would evidence that a person was not insured be relevant to prove negligence or the absence of negligence?

2. FRE 411 explicitly provides that evidence of liability insurance may be admissible for purposes other than showing negligence or wrongful conduct, such as proof of agency, ownership, or control, or bias or prejudice of a witness. Would the evidence be admissible under CEC 1155 if offered for these purposes? [**Example: J-23**].

3. What if a reference to insurance is included in an admission of liability? Immediately after a hunting accident in which the defendant shot the plaintiff, the defendant says, "Don't worry, if your insurance doesn't cover this, mine will." The exclusion of this statement was upheld in *Meneta v. Williams*, 259 Cal.App.2d 56 (1968).

4. Don't confuse life insurance with liability insurance. Evidence that an accused is the beneficiary of a life insurance policy on the life of a murder victim would be relevant evidence of motive. [**Examples: F-56, K-103**].

Chapter Nine

Plea Bargaining in Criminal Cases

Focus on CEC 1153

1. As previously noted, CEC 1153 is abrogated in criminal cases by operation of Proposition 8. The section also precludes use of plea offers in subsequent civil suits, however, and its application in this setting would be unaffected by Proposition 8. [**Example: J-20**].
2. FRE 410 prohibits any use of a plea of *nolo contendere* in a subsequent civil or criminal proceeding. There is no parallel exclusion in the California Evidence Code. California Penal Code §1016 provides that in felony cases, a plea of *nolo contendere* shall be the same as a plea of guilty for all purposes. In misdemeanor cases, however, Penal Code §1016 provides that the plea and any admissions made in offering the plea may not be used as an admission in any civil suit based on the act upon which the criminal prosecution is based. CEC 1300 creates a hearsay exception for felony criminal judgments when offered in a civil action, "whether or not the judgment was based on a plea of nolo contendere."
3. Note that CEC 1153, unlike FRE 410, precludes use of plea offers by any party, not just when offered against the defendant. Thus it would appear to preclude a defendant's offer of a rejected plea offer as evidence of "consciousness of innocence."
4. Like FRE 410, CEC 1153 is an absolute prohibition of use of the evidence for any purpose. It does not even contain the limited exceptions contained in FRE 410. Thus, the policy against admission of this evidence appears to have less flexibility than the other rules of exclusion based upon extrinsic policy. Nonethless, the California Court of Appeal, in reviewing the conviction of Sirhan Sirhan for the murder of Robert F. Kennedy, found a way around it. During Sirhan's trial, in the absence of the jury, defense counsel advised the

court of a disagreement between himself and the defendant, and stated that the defendant wished to address the court. Sirhan then stated he wanted to plead guilty and be executed. The court said it could not permit him to do this without a reason. Sirhan then stated, "I killed Robert Kennedy willfully, premeditatively, and with twenty years of malice aforethought, that is why." A plea was not accepted, and the trial continued after the defendant and his counsel resolved their differences. At a later point in the trial, Sirhan testified in his own defense, and stated he did not remember shooting Kennedy. The prosecutor then asked, on cross-examination, "Well, the other day right here in this courtroom did you not say, 'I killed Robert Kennedy willfully, premeditatively, and with twenty years of malice aforethought,' did you say that?" Sirhan answered, "Yes, sir, I did."

On appeal, the court rejected an argument that the prosecutor's cross-examination violated CEC 1153. The court explained:

> The obvious purpose of the statutes is to promote the public interest by encouraging the settlement of criminal cases without the necessity of a trial.... In view of that purpose it seems clear that the Legislature intended to exclude solely withdrawn guilty pleas and *bona fide* offers to plead guilty and did not intend to exclude outbursts by an angry defendant during the trial even if accompanied by an expression of a desire to plead guilty. Such outbursts, of course, would not lead to the settlement of the criminal case without a trial and ordinarily would not end the trial but instead would merely disrupt it. Here, it is apparent that Sirhan's admission was made during such an outburst rather than during a bona fide offer to plead guilty.

People v. Sirhan, 7 Cal.3d 710, 745–46 (1972).

Part III

Character Evidence

Introduction

A Road Map

Character evidence presents the most complex and difficult challenge in the study of Evidence. It is also the area where we encounter the most differences between the Federal Rules of Evidence and the California Evidence Code. Proposition 8 complicates the situation somewhat, often requiring a distinction between civil and criminal cases which is not apparent from the Code itself.

The following chart should be used as a "road-map" through this difficult terrain. It compares federal and California rules governing the admissibility of the two major forms of character evidence (reputation or opinion evidence and evidence of specific acts) for each of the major purposes for which the evidence may be offered. The first category deals with evidence offered when character is directly in issue, where we are not drawing an inference from the character evidence, but the character itself is an element of the cause of action. For example, we want to prove that a mother is a poor parent in a child custody dispute, or we want to show the plaintiff suffered little damage in a libel action because everyone thought he was a sleaze-ball even before he was libeled. The remaining categories will be dealt with in each of the succeeding chapters.

Purpose Evidence is Offered	Reputation or Opinion Evidence	Evidence of Specific Acts
1. Character is directly in issue.	CAL: YES (CEC 1100) FED: YES (FRE 405(b))	CAL: YES (CEC 1100) FED: YES (FRE 405(b))
2. To show something other than "character": Preparation, Intent, Knowledge, Opportunity Identity, Motive, Plan or to Negate Accident or Mistake.	CAL: NO (CEC 1101(a)) FED: NO (FRE 404(a))	CAL: YES (1101(b)) FED: YES (FRE 404(b))
3. To Show Conduct or Propensity of Defendant in Criminal Cases.	CAL: YES [GOOD-BAD] (CEC 1102) OR REBUTTAL OF ATTACK ON VICTIM'S CHAR. (CEC 1103(b)) FED: YES [GOOD-BAD] OR REBUTTAL OF ATTACK ON VICTIM'S CHAR. (FRE 404(a))	CAL: YES, FOR SEX OFFENSES (CEC 1108); DOMESTIC VIOLENCE (CEC 1109); REBUTTAL OF ATTACK ON VICTIM'S CHAR. (CEC 1103(b)) AND CROSS-EXAM OF CHARACTER WITNESS. FED: YES, FOR SEXUAL ASSAULT (FRE 413,415); CHILD MOLESTATION (FRE 414, 415) AND CROSS-EXAM OF CHARACTER WITNESS.
4. To Show Conduct or Propensity of Non-Rape Victims.	CAL: YES [BAD-GOOD] (CEC 1103(a)) FED: YES [BAD-GOOD] (FRE 404(a))	CAL: YES [BAD-GOOD] (CEC 1103(a)) FED: CROSS EXAM ONLY (FRE 405(a))
5. To Show Conduct or Propensity of Rape Victims.	CAL: NO (CEC 1103(c)) FED: NO (FRE 412(a))	CAL: NO [EXCEPT WITH DEF.] (CEC 1103(c)) FED: NO [EXCEPT WITH DEF.] (FRE 412(b))
6. To Show Conduct or Propensity in Civil Cases.	CAL: NO (CEC 1101(a)), EXCEPT LOSS OF CONSORTIUM (CEC 1106) FED: NO (FRE 404(a))	CAL: NO (CEC 1101(a)), EXCEPT LOSS OF CONSORTIUM (CEC 1106) FED: NO (FRE 404(a)), EXCEPT SEXUAL ASSAULT OR CHILD MOLESTATION (FRE 415)

Purpose Evidence is Offered	Reputation or Opinion Evidence	Evidence of Specific Acts
7. To Show Credibility of Witness [Honesty / Veracity].	CAL: CIVIL: YES [BAD-GOOD] (CEC 790); CRIM: YES (PROP. 8) FED: YES [BAD-GOOD] (FRE 608(a))	CONVICTIONS: CAL: CIVIL: FELONY (CEC 788) CRIM: MORAL TURPITUDE (PROP. 8) FED: FELONY OR DISHONESTY (FRE 608(b)) NON-CONVICTIONS: CAL: CIVIL: NO (CEC 787) CRIM: YES (PROP. 8) FED: CROSS EXAM ONLY (FRE 608(b))

Chapter Ten

The Character-Propensity Rule and Its Exceptions

Focus on CEC 1100 and 1101

1. Clearly, evidence of character may be relevant to prove the conduct with which a defendant is charged in either civil or criminal cases. In seeking to prove that the defendant stole a wallet, his reputation as a dishonest person and his two prior convictions for stealing the wallets of other victims certainly "have a tendency in reason" to make it more likely he committed the charged theft. In seeking to prove a defendant caused an accident by driving too fast, his reputation as a speed demon and his six previous speeding tickets "have a tendency in reason" to make it more likely he was speeding when the accident occurred. Thus, CEC 1101(a) excludes relevant evidence, and would be abrogated by Section 28(d) of Proposition 8 in criminal cases. In *People v. Ewoldt*, 7 Cal.4th 380 (1994), the California Supreme Court ruled that CEC 1101(a) was "saved" because the legislature re-enacted it in 1986 by a two-thirds vote. Thus, it comes within Prop. 8 exception no. 2, *supra*. [The re-enactment was part of an amendment to Section 1101(b), which added to the string of examples of when character evidence can be admitted to show a fact other than disposition, when evidence is offered to show "whether a defendant in a prosecution for an unlawful sexual act or attempted unlawful sexual act did not reasonably and in good faith believe the victim consented."] Section 9 of Article IV of the California constitution provides that a "section of a statute may not be amended unless the section is re-enacted as amended."

The *Ewoldt* Court then proceeded to apply CEC 1101 to a case in which the defendant was accused of sexually molesting his young step-daughter, including an incident in which she awoke as he was fondling her breasts. The defendant claimed that he was covering her with a blanket. The prosecution presented testimony of the victim's older sister, who testified that the defendant had previously molested her in the same fashion, claiming he was "straightening up the covers." The Court upheld admission of the prior specific acts on the ground that they came within the CEC 1101(b) exception to show a "common design or plan." In doing so, the Court overruled a prior precedent which excluded evidence of similar misconduct to show a common design or plan unless "the charged and uncharged acts are part of a single, continuing conception or plot." *People v. Tassell*, 36 Cal.3d 77 (1984).

The *Ewoldt* case was decided prior to the enactment of CEC 1108, which now creates a broad exception to CEC 1101 for sexual offenses, permitting evidence of the defendant's commission of another sexual offense to show propensity. [**Example: C-15**].

2. In the *Ewoldt* case, the defendant denied that he did the alleged *act* of molestation, not that he lacked the requisite intent. In fact, he offered to stipulate "that if the jury finds that the defendant was present and committed the various acts which are the subject of these charges...he did so with the requisite specific intent." *Id.* at n.7. The Court made it clear that proof of a "common design or plan" was admissible to show commission of the charged acts. If its only relevance were to show intent, the Court noted, it should have been excluded under CEC 352. The Court explained the importance of which of the CEC 1101(b) purposes permits the admission of the evidence to the subsequent balancing of probative weight vs. potential for prejudice:

> Our holding does not mean that evidence of a defendant's similar uncharged acts that demonstrate the existence of a common design or plan will be admissible in all (or even most) criminal prosecutions. In many cases, the prejudicial effect of such evidence would outweigh its probative value, because the evidence would merely be cumulative regarding an issue that was not reasonably subject to dispute. [Citation omitted]. This is so because evidence of a common design or plan is admissible only to establish that the defendant engaged in the conduct alleged to constitute the charged offense, not to prove other matters, such as the defendant's intent or identity as to the charged offense. For example, in most prosecutions for crimes such as burglary and robbery, it is beyond dispute that the charged offense was committed by someone; the primary issue to be determined is whether the defendant was the perpetrator of that crime. Thus, in such circumstances, evidence that the defendant committed uncharged offenses that were sufficiently similar to the charged offense to demonstrate a common design or plan (but not sufficiently distinctive to establish identity) ordinarily would be inadmissible. Al-

though such evidence is relevant to demonstrate that, assuming the defendant was present at the scene of the crime, the defendant engaged in the conduct alleged to constitute the charged offense, if it is beyond dispute that the alleged crime occurred, such evidence would be merely cumulative and the prejudicial effect of the evidence of uncharged acts would outweigh its probative value. In ruling upon the admissibility of evidence of uncharged acts, therefore, it is imperative that the trial court determine specifically what the proffered evidence is offered to prove, so that the probative value of the evidence can be evaluated for that purpose.

7 Cal.4th at 405–406.

3. The *Ewoldt* Court makes it clear that where the purpose of the prior act is to prove identity of the perpetrator of the charged act, even greater similarity between the crimes is required than would suffice to show a common plan or scheme. [**Example: D-8**]. The unique similarities in the method of committing a series of crimes actually led to the identification of a murder suspect by the police in one of the most amazing murder cases in California history. Eddie Wein was convicted of six counts of rape in Los Angeles in 1957. Each of the rapes was committed in a similar manner. Wein would answer a newspaper ad for the sale of some household article. If he found the victim alone in her home, he would interrupt their conversation by claiming that the watch stem had fallen out of his watch. The victim would instinctively bend down to help him look for it, and he would then grab her from behind, bind her hands with wire, and force her into acts of sexual perversion. Wein was convicted and sentenced to death under the same "Little Lindbergh" law used in the notorious case of Caryl Chessman, whereby the movement of a victim was treated as kidnapping, a capital offense. *People v. Wein*, 50 Cal.2d 383 (1958). Wein's sentence was later commuted to life imprisonment by Governor Pat Brown, who had the same objection to Wein's death sentence that he had to Chessman's. He simply did not think kidnapping not resulting in a death should be a capital offense. Brown later wrote that the commutation of Eddie Wein's sentence was "the worst mistake I ever made," and in a remarkable book he explained why:

> I'd been practicing law in Los Angeles for almost eight years when in November, 1975 I boarded an airplane for one of my frequent trips to San Francisco. The man in the seat next to me was a stranger, but he obviously knew who I was. "Have you seen this?" he asked with what sounded like contempt, handing me the front page of that morning's *Los Angeles Times*. "Trademark and a Memory Jail Man," said the headline he was pointing to. I read with growing horror how

Eddie Wein's luck had once again run out.... "A unique 'trademark' which helped to almost send a convicted rapist to the gas chamber 19 years ago, plus the sharp memory of a retired police detective, has put Edward Simon Wein back in custody again—this time, on suspicion of murder," the story began. "For Wein, now 51, who was released on parole Sept. 16, 1974, after serving 17 years in prison for sexually assaulting at least six Los Angeles-area women, his arrest yesterday, like his capture in 1956, turned on a once-in-a-million happenstance. But, in both instances, it was his trademark—putting his victims off guard by pretending to have lost his watch stem—that made him stand out and assured that he would be remembered almost two decades later...."

The *Times* story went on to tell how a former LAPD detective named Robert Wright, retired for just two months, went to the regular monthly luncheon held by a group of police colleagues and heard the details of two disturbingly similar recent crimes in the area around Los Angeles International Airport. A fifty-two year old Westchester housewife had been found dead, bound hand and foot, stabbed several times with a sharp instrument, strangled and drowned in her bathtub. In the second case, a forty-year-old Palms woman had narrowly survived death when she was sexually attacked, bound, beaten and stabbed in the neck by a middle-aged man who had answered an ad which she had put up in a neighborhood supermarket, offering a bed for sale. Hearing this, something began to stir in Wright's memory, and when he said that the murdered woman had also recently advertised some furniture for sale on a supermarket bulletin board, a light went on. Although he hadn't personally worked on the Wein case, Wright recalled the details. "We had a case back in the fifties of a man who went to the houses of women who had placed newspaper classified ads for things to sell," he said. "I can't remember his name, but this guy had a way of getting physical control over the victims, by pretending to drop his watch stem. When the women bent over to help him look for it, he grabbed them from behind."

Wright's detective friend was amazed. "Hell, that's what the suspect did in the Palms case!" he told him. Together, they sent off a request to the Adult Authority, looking for a recent parolee who had used the watch-stem gambit. Back came a name—Eddie Wein, paroled in 1974, now living with relatives in Rancho Park, close to both Palms and Westchester. A witness had seen a man leave the home of the murdered woman and enter a car: his description matched Wein and a car he had borrowed. Wein was arrested that night, and booked on suspicion of murder. The next day, the Palms victim picked him out of a police line-up; charges of attempted murder, rape and sexual perversion were also filed.

I finished the story, including a short paragraph about my successive commutations of Wein's sentences that made his parole possible, and handed the paper back to my seatmate. He must have seen on my face the distress I was feeling, because he was silent for the rest of the short trip. As for myself, I was racked with guilt and doubt. I had made mistakes before—anybody who makes decisions as part of his job finds out later that some of them were wrong—but this one had cost a woman her life. I honestly think that if, at that moment, I could have somehow traded the lives of all twenty-three of the people whose death sentences I'd commuted for the life of that Westchester woman, I would have done so.

Edmund (Pat) Brown, *Public Justice, Private Mercy: A Governor's Education on Death Row,* pp. 101–103 (1989). Clearly, the six rapes of which Wein was convicted in 1957 would be admissible to prove his identity as the perpetrator of the Palms rape. What about the Westchester murder?

3. When a prosecutor offers uncharged acts or conduct pursuant to CEC 1101(b) or FRE 404(b), the reason they are "uncharged" is frequently because the statute of limitations has elapsed. One of the purposes for the statute of limitations is to protect an accused from having to defend against allegations of events long after they happened, when memories have faded and evidence has disappeared. Is the lapse of time a significant factor for the judge to weigh in determining the admissibility of uncharged conduct under CEC 1101(b)? Does it affect the probative value of the evidence under CEC 352? Is "fairness" to the defendant a relevant consideration in assessing probative value? If a witness claims a vivid memory of a sexual incident twenty years before, and can even corroborate it with a contemporaneous diary entry, would its strong probative value be undercut by the defendant's lack of access to evidence to corroborate his denial?

4. Both FRE 404(b) and CEC 1101(b) recognize "exceptions" for evidence of other crimes, wrongs and acts. They do *not* open the door to evidence in the form of reputation or opinion. Thus, even if the purpose of the evidence was to show dishonest intent, one could not offer evidence of the defendant's bad reputation for dishonesty. [**Example: K-23**].

5. In *Huddleston v. United States,* 485 U.S. 681 (1988), the U.S. Supreme Court held that proof of whether the other crimes, wrongs or acts occurred was a

question of conditional relevancy, and should be submitted to the jury under FRE 104(b), upon submission of evidence sufficient to support a finding. Precisely the same procedure would be followed under the California Evidence Code. CEC 403(a)(4) requires the court to find evidence sufficient to support a finding where "[t]he proffered evidence is of...conduct of a particular person and the preliminary fact is whether that person...so conducted himself."

6. Where liability is based upon negligence, whether in civil or criminal cases, prior incidents of carelessness cannot be offered to show a propensity for negligence, nor can prior acts of carefulness be offered to show one is a cautious person. CEC 1104. [**Examples: B-11, B-19, J-5, J-11**]. But the exceptions in CEC 1101(b) are available when the evidence is relevant for some other purpose. [**Examples: B-5, F-59, F-63**].

7. Acts *subsequent* to the charged conduct are also excluded by CEC 1101(a), but may come within the CEC 1101(b) exceptions, such as to show motive. [**Example: F-75**].

Chapter Eleven

Propensity Evidence in Sexual Assault and Domestic Violence Cases

Focus on CEC 1108 and 1109

1. Note that FRE 413 and 414 treat sexual assault and child molestation separately. If a defendant is accused of child molestation, the prosecution may not offer prior offenses of sexual assault against adults pursuant to FRE 414. If a defendant is charged with sexual assault, however, prior sexual assaults are admissible under FRE 413, whether the victim was an adult or a child. If the evidence is being admitted to show propensity, would a rapist be more likely to molest a child than one who was not a rapist? CEC 1108 lumps all sexual offenses together. The Penal Code offenses listed in CEC 1108(d)(1) include sexual battery, rape, unlawful sexual intercourse with persons under 18, spousal rape, sodomy, lewd acts, oral copulation, seduction of minors, child sexual abuse, forcible sexual penetration, possession or distribution of child pornography, sexual exploitation of children, and annoying or molesting children under 18. [**Examples: C-15, L-72**]. Unless the defendant is charged with one of the specified offenses, however, the CEC 1108 exception has no application. [**Example: G-28**].

2. In *People v. Falsetta*, 21 Cal.4th 903 (1999), the California Supreme Court upheld CEC 1108 against a challenge that the admission of propensity evidence violated the defendant's right to due process of law. The Court noted that by expressly allowing the judge to exclude the evidence under CEC 352, Section 1108 provided a safeguard against undue prejudice that saved it from the due process challenge.

3. CEC 1108 only applies to a criminal action. There is no parallel exception for civil cases such as FRE 415 under the federal rules, nor is "propensity" ev-

idence admissible in sexual harassment cases. [**Examples: H-27, H-36**]. But CEC 1101(b) exceptions might admit prior acts of sexual harassment to show intent or plan. (The exception to negate reasonable belief in consent is limited to criminal prosecutions). [**Example: H-40**].

4. CEC 1109 was enacted in response to the O.J. Simpson trial, to extend the rationale of CEC 1108 to cases of "domestic violence." If the defendant is accused of "an offense involving domestic violence," then evidence of any other domestic violence will not be excluded by CEC 1101. [**Example: K-12**]. It may be excluded by exercising the judge's discretion under CEC 352, however. "Domestic violence" is defined as it is in Penal Code Section 13700, which provides:

> "Domestic violence" means abuse committed against an adult or a minor who is a spouse, former spouse, cohabitant, former cohabitant, or person with whom the suspect has had a child or is having or has had a dating or engagement relationship. For purposes of this subdivision, "cohabitant" means two unrelated adult persons living together for a substantial period of time, resulting in some permanency of relationship. Factors that may determine whether persons are cohabiting include, but are not limited to, (1) sexual relations between the parties while sharing the same living quarters, (2) sharing of income or expenses, (3) joint use or ownership of property, (4) whether the parties hold themselves out as husband and wife, (5) the continuity of the relationship, and (6) the length of the relationship.

[**Examples: K-24, K-43, K-117/119**].

CHAPTER TWELVE

PROOF OF DEFENDANT'S AND VICTIM'S CHARACTER

Focus on CEC 1102 and 1103(a) and (b)

1. Under CEC 1102, the defendant who opts to put his character "in issue" can offer evidence of good character in the form of opinion or reputation, and the prosecution can then rebut it with opinion or reputation evidence of bad character. The evidence is limited to *relevant* traits of character, however. [**Example: G-57**]. The real risk for the defendant, however, is the kind of cross-examination of his good-character witnesses permitted by *Michelson v. United States*, 335 U.S. 469 (1948). The right to conduct *Michelson* cross-examination in federal cases is preserved by FRE 405. The rule modifies *Michelson*, which declared:

> Since the whole inquiry...is calculated to ascertain the general talk of people about the defendant, rather than the witness' own knowledge of him, the form of inquiry, "Have you heard?" has general approval, and "Do you know" is not allowed.

335 U.S. at 482. With respect to *opinion* witnesses, though, the "Do you know" form of question was generally permitted. The Advisory Committee Note to FRE 405 indicates that "[t]he fact is, of course, that these distinctions are of slight if any practical significance; the second sentence of subdivision (a) eliminates them as a factor in formulating questions."

These distinctions *are* preserved under the California Evidence Code, however. The reputation witness must be asked, "Have you heard?" *People v. Marsh*, 58 Cal.2d 732, 745 (1962). Only opinion witnesses can be asked, "Do you know?", but in *People v. Hurd*, 5 Cal.App.3d 865 (1970), the court held it was not error to allow "Have you heard" questions to be addressed to an opinion witness. [**Examples: G-58, H-29**].

From a tactical standpoint, what can counsel do to minimize the risks of cross-examination of character witnesses? Can their testimony be limited to a time frame that excludes prior arrests or convictions? Can their testimony be limited to specific traits of character as to which some prior incidents would be irrelevant?

2. The option given to the defendant in CEC 1102 to present evidence of his good character is only available in a criminal action. And it does not permit proof of specific acts of good conduct, although this limitation may have been abrogated by Proposition 8. [**Example: D-31**]. Likewise, the option in FRE 404(a)(1) is only available to the "accused" in a criminal prosecution.

3. The accused can also attack the bad character of a victim, but under FRE 404(a) the attack is limited to opinion or reputation witnesses, and may not include specific instances of conduct. CEC 1103(a), however, allows the victim to be attacked with specific instances of conduct as well as opinion or reputation. The risks of mounting such an attack are substantial, however. Not only does it open the door to rebuttal evidence of the victim's *good* character, if the attack relates to the victim's character for violence or a trait of character related to violence, the prosecutor can rebut with evidence of the *defendant's* bad character, including specific instances of conduct. CEC 1103(b). By virtue of an amendment to FRE 404(a)(1) adopted in 2000, an attack on the victim's character also opens the door to an attack on the same trait of character for the defendant. But unlike CEC 1103(a), both the attack and the response are limited to opinion and reputation witnesses.

CHAPTER THIRTEEN

RAPE VICTIMS AND THE RAPE SHIELD LAW

Focus on CEC 1103(a), 1106, 782, 783

1. The "rape shield" law protects the complaining witness of a sexual assault from the admission of evidence of his or her prior sexual conduct in order to prove consent. FRE 412 governs both criminal and civil cases, while the California Evidence Code has two separate rules, CEC 1103(c) for criminal cases, and CEC 1106 for civil cases. Cross examination of the victim is also treated separately for criminal cases in CEC 782, and for civil cases in CEC 783. [**Examples:** L-15, L-18]. The "rape shield" law only protects the victim in the case being tried, however. Protection would not extend to other victims testifying to prior incidents which are not charged. [**Examples:** L-84, L-98]. The "civil" rape shield in CEC 1106 applies to cases of sexual harassment. [**Example:** H-14].
2. Unlike the federal rule, CEC 1103(c) provides that the "rape shield" is not available "where the crime is alleged to have occurred in a local detention facility... or in a state prison." Why should the victims of prison rapes, either by guards or by other prisoners, have less protection than rape victims who are not confined?
3. Both FRE 412 and CEC 1103(c) permit evidence of the victim's sexual activity with the defendant. But CEC 1103(c) exempts *sexual conduct* with the defendant, while FRE 412(b)(1)(B) exempts *sexual behavior* "with respect to" the defendant. The difference can be significant, since the Advisory Committee Note to FRE 412 provides that "the word 'behavior' should be construed to include activities of the mind, such as fantasies or dreams." Thus, the federal rule would permit the defense to inquire into the victims sexual fantasies with respect to the defendant, while the California rule would not.
4. CEC 1103(c)(4) provides that if the prosecutor elicits testimony suggesting a *lack* of prior sexual experience by the complaining witness, the defendant

can offer evidence in rebuttal. Thus, if the victim testified she had never had sexual intercourse before she was raped by the defendant, the defendant could offer evidence of prior sexual intercourse with others. Other sexual activity may also be relevant to show a source of injuries or semen other than the alleged sexual activity with the defendant. [**Examples:** L-42, L-90].

5. If the evidence of sexual activity is not offered to show consent, but is offered to attack the credibility of the victim, it's admissibility is governed by CEC 782 and 783.

Evidence of prior false accusations by the victim will ordinarily be admitted. In *People v. Wall,* 95 Cal.App.3d 978 (1979), the Court of Appeal held that prior incidents with others showing a willingness to fabricate in retaliation are not excluded by the California "rape shield" law.

6. The four day trial of sportscaster Marv Albert in 1997 for forcible sodomy in Virginia, which ended in a plea bargain, ignited a lively national debate about the "rape shield" laws. The prosecution called several "surprise" witnesses to describe prior sexual trysts with Albert, while he was precluded from challenging the victim's credibility with evidence that she acted vengefully toward other ex-boyfriends. *See* Gebeaut, "Shield a Prosecution Sword," ABA Journal, December, 1997, p.36.

The California Evidence Code seeks to foreclose the mid-trial surprises which characterized the Albert trial. CEC 1108 requires the prosecution to disclose predisposition evidence it intends to offer against the defendant 30 days in advance. In addition, CEC 782 and 783 require a written motion and offer of proof before the defendant may challenge the credibility of the victim with evidence involving sexual conduct.

7. The effectiveness of "rape shield" laws in encouraging victims to report rapes is open to question. The F.B.I. reported that in 1975, 1 out of 7 forcible rapes were reported. In 1995, after "rape shield" laws were in place in most American jurisdictions, the F.B.I. reported that 1 out of 7 forcible rapes were reported. What other disincentives continue to operate to discourage rape victims from reporting the crime?

8. Rape victims are also protected with a cloak of anonymity in California. The charging document will refer to the victim as "Jane Doe" or "John Doe," and the victim will not be required to divulge his or her true name when testifying. Cal. Pen. Code §293.5.

CHAPTER FOURTEEN

EVIDENCE OF HABIT

Focus on CEC 1105

1. When "habit" is used to prove conduct in conformity with the habit, the habit is being used to suggest propensity. Can the rule against using character evidence to show propensity be evaded simply by calling it evidence of "habit", rather than evidence of "character"?
2. FRE 406 allows evidence of "the routine practice of an organization." Would CEC 1105 let the same evidence in as evidence of "custom"?
3. FRE 406 explicitly abrogates common law limitations on habit evidence that permitted it only when eye witnesses were unavailable, and required corroboration of the routine practice of an organization. The Law Revision Commission comment to CEC 1105 makes it clear that the "no eyewitness" requirement is eliminated, but what about the corroboration requirement?
4. The comment to FRE 406 suggests that evidence of "intemperate habits" is generally excluded when offered as proof of drunkenness in accident cases. Wouldn't the practice of stopping at the same bar for two beers every night on the way home from work qualify as a "habit"? Should regular use of illicit drugs be treated differently than regular use of alcohol? In *People v. Humphries,* 185 Cal.App.3d 1315 (1986), the court held that it was error to exclude evidence that a prosecution witness was a habitual drug user to prove he ingested PCP on the day he witnessed the crime. [**Example:** J-7].
5. CEC 1104 excludes evidence of "a trait of a person's character with respect to care or skill" to prove the quality of his conduct on a specific occasion. In *People v. Cabral,* 141 Cal.App.3d 148 (1983), a chiropractor was accused of manslaughter when his patient died as a result of uncontrolled epileptic seizures. The parents of the patient testified that the defendant advised them to discontinue the use of anti-convulsant medications. Relying on CEC 1104, the trial court excluded evidence that the defendant regularly declined to interfere with medication prescribed by other doctors, including the testimony

of other patients that they were so advised. On appeal, the court held that the evidence should have been admitted under CEC 1105, as evidence of habit or custom. [**Example: D-35**].

6. In the trial of *People v. O.J. Simpson*, the defense offered evidence that Detective Mark Fuhrman had "covered up" police misconduct by other officers in prior incidents to show that the Los Angeles Police Department had a "custom" under which police officers were expected to lie if necessary to protect each other. The trial judge sustained an objection under CEC 352 to exclude the evidence. In *People v. Memro*, 38 Cal.3d 658, 681 (1985), the California Supreme Court upheld a discovery request for evidence regarding police interrogation in previous cases, saying:

> Plainly, evidence that the interrogating officers had a custom or habit of obtaining confessions by violence, force, threat or unlawful aggressive behavior would have been admissible on the issue of whether the confession had been coerced.

7. Can "habit" be established by opinion evidence, or must it be shown by repeated specific instances? Would the sufficiency of the evidence to show "habit" be resolved as a matter of conditional relevancy under CEC 403, or would it be determined by the judge pursuant to CEC 405?

Chapter Fifteen

Character for Truthfulness

Focus on CEC 786, 787, 788 and 790

1. The only character trait which is relevant to challenge the credibility of a witness is "truthfulness or untruthfulness" under FRE 608(a), or "honesty or veracity, or their opposites" under CEC 780(a) and 786. [**Examples: A-35, A-39, D-35, D-37, E-58, H-14, H-41, K-49, K-57, K-99, L-100**].
2. FRE 608(a)(2) allows reputation or opinion evidence of truthful character to support a witness only after the witness' character has been attacked. CEC 790 imposes the same restriction, but would be abrogated in criminal cases by Proposition 8 since it excludes relevant evidence. Could the trial judge achieve the same end in a criminal case by applying CEC 352? If the truthfulness of the witness has not been attacked, then evidence of his truthful character would have slight probative value and would necessitate undue consumption of time. [**Example: H-25**].
3. With the exception of criminal convictions, specific acts are not admissible to show bad character for truthfulness or honesty under both FRE 608(b) and CEC 787. [**Examples: H-85, K-99**]. Once again, however, CEC 787 excludes relevant evidence, so Proposition 8 would prevent its application in criminal cases. The trial judge can exclude the evidence under CEC 352, but only if its probative value is substantially outweighed. The federal rule permits specific instances to be probed on cross-examination of the witness, however. Note that this is essentially different from the cross-examination of character witnesses under *Michelson*. There, a witness is testifying to the good character of the accused, and is asked if he has heard of some misconduct by the accused. Under FRE 608(b), the witness is asked about his *own* misconduct. For example, "Is it true you were expelled from college for cheating on a final examination?" FRE 608(b) prohibits any extrinsic evidence. Therefore, if the wit-

ness answered "no" to the preceding question, he could not be impeached with a certified transcript showing he had, in fact, been expelled for cheating. In California criminal cases, Proposition 8 would allow both the cross-examination and the extrinsic evidence, although the trial judge would have discretion to exclude it under CEC 352. [**Examples: A-49, F-83**].

4. Carefully distinguish evidence of bias from evidence of bad character. If the inquiry on cross-examination is to show the witness' *bias,* the question as well as the extrinsic evidence would not be precluded, even in a civil case. [**Examples: A-31, A-41, D-41, E-40, E-43, E-63, E-65, F-25, G-14, G-66, H-47, H-51, J-79, J-81, K-31, K-55, K-65, L-78**]. In *People v. O.J. Simpson,* for example, the defense was permitted to cross-examine Detective Mark Fuhrman about his use of the "N-word" not to attack his character, but to show his bias toward black persons. When he denied the use of the word, extrinsic evidence of prior tape-recorded interviews in which he used the word repeatedly was admitted to impeach him. However, Judge Ito exercised his discretion under CEC 352 and did not allow the tapes to be played, but merely allowed a summary of their contents.

5. FRE 609 sets up four different standards for the admission of prior convictions to impeach the credibility of a witness:

(1) If the crime involved dishonesty or false statement, whether it is a felony or a misdemeanor, it is always admissible. There is no discretion to exclude it, even under FRE 403.

(2) If the crime is any other felony offense, and the witness is anyone other than the accused, the judge applies the normal FRE 403 standard, and can exclude it only if its probative value is substantially outweighed by its potential for prejudice.

(3) If the crime is any other felony offense, and the witness is the accused, the judge must admit it if its probative value outweighs its potential for prejudice. This is a different standard than FRE 403, requiring a more even handed balancing without a thumb on the scale in favor of admission by requiring *substantial* risk of prejudice to exclude it.

(4) If the felony conviction is more than ten years old, it must be excluded unless the court determines the probative value substantially outweighs the prejudicial effect. This reverses the normal FRE 403 standard.

Under CEC 788, the same standard will always be applied under CEC 352 to balance probative value against prejudicial effect. But the nature of the convictions permitted will vary significantly between civil and criminal cases. Civil cases in California are governed by the judicial interpretation of CEC 788 prior to the enactment of Proposition 8.

6. In *People v. Beagle*, 6 Cal.3d 441 (1972), the Court identified five circumstances to be considered in balancing the probative value of prior convictions offered pursuant to CEC 788 against the potential for prejudice. First, convictions with little direct bearing on veracity should be excluded. The Court suggested that only convictions involving dishonesty are probative of lack of veracity. Second, even convictions involving dishonesty should be excluded if they are remote in time and the witness has led a blameless life since the conviction. Third, if the conviction involves conduct identical or similar to conduct the witness is accused of in the trial itself, it should be excluded because of the grave risk that the jury will misuse it as propensity evidence. Fourth, if convictions are numerous, the court should restrict the number used to avoid the prejudice inherent in large numbers of convictions. Finally, convictions should be excluded if they will deter the witness from testifying, and the judge concludes it is more important to let the jury have the benefit of the testimony. While these guidelines were formulated with criminal trials in mind, they all have potential application in civil cases as well, and the California Supreme Court has made it clear they apply to all witnesses and in all trials. *People v. Woodard*, 23 Cal.3d 329, 338 (1979). [**Examples: B-57, J-20**].

7. Proposition 8 contains both a constitutional prohibition against the exclusion of relevant evidence in criminal cases (Art.I, Section 28(d)), and a constitutional command that "any felony conviction of any person...shall subsequently be used without limitation for purposes of impeachment...in any criminal proceeding." (Art.I, Section 28(f)). In *People v. Castro*, 38 Cal.3d 301 (1985), however, the Court recognized two "limitations" on the use of prior convictions for purposes of impeachment in criminal proceedings: the federal constitutional protection of due process of law, and the discretion of trial judges to exclude prejudicial evidence under CEC 352.

Due process, the Court declared, requires the exclusion of convictions that do not involve "moral turpitude." To permit the fact finder to consider convictions not related to veracity would deprive the accused of a fair trial in which only relevant and competent evidence is considered in determining his guilt. "Moral turpitude" was defined as a readiness to do evil, including crimes of violence and brutality. The Court ruled that Castro's conviction of simple heroin possession did not involve moral turpitude and could not be used to impeach him, although a conviction for distribution of heroin, or even possession with intent to distribute, might. Felonies subsequently held *not* to involve moral turpitude include statutory rape, involuntary manslaughter, simple assault, simple battery, felony child endangerment, and possession of marijuana. Felonies based upon strict liability or negligence have generally been excluded.

Noting that Section 28(d) of Proposition 8 preserved the trial judge's discretion under CEC 352, the *Castro* Court read the "without limitation" clause of Section 28(f) as a rejection of the mandatory limitations imposed by *People v. Beagle*, but not of the judicial discretion applied by judges prior to *Beagle*. *Beagle* itself, the Court ruled, should still guide the trial judge's exercise of discretion, but none of the *Beagle* guidelines would *mandate* exclusion of prior convictions in criminal cases. In *People v. Clair*, 2 Cal.4th 629, 655 (1992), the court held even a conviction involving moral turpitude (voluntary manslaughter) could be excluded in a criminal case after Proposition 8 under CEC 352, if it was remote in time and the witness had led a blameless life since the conviction. [**Examples: A-37, E-63, E-65, F-77, G-60, K-29, L-108**].

8. If the witness does not acknowledge a prior conviction, it must be proven by the judgment of the court which rendered it. That judgment, however, would be hearsay. While there is a hearsay exception in the California Evidence Code for felony judgments, it is only applicable in civil cases. CEC 1300. Thus, CEC 788 itself creates a hearsay exception, but only for a judgment of a *felony* conviction. While a misdemeanor conviction might also be for a crime of moral turpitude or dishonesty, and thus *relevant* in a criminal case, the judgment of conviction of the misdemeanor would be excluded as *hearsay*. *People v. Wheeler*, 4 Cal.4th 284, 299 (1992). The facts underlying the misdemeanor conviction might be admissible as relevant evidence under Proposition 8 in a criminal case to challenge the credibility of a witness, but they would have to be proven by percipient witnesses rather than by the judgment of conviction. Such evidence could be vulnerable to exclusion under CEC 352 because of undue consumption of time.

9. Ordinarily, the admissibility of prior convictions will be litigated in a pretrial motion in limine, before the witness is called to testify. But in *People v. Collins*, 42 Cal.3d 378 (1986), the court held that the trial judge could postpone ruling on the admissibility of a prior conviction until after the defendant testifies, relying upon the similar ruling of the U.S. Supreme Court in *Luce v. United States*, 469 U.S. 38 (1984). If the judge rules the conviction may be used, and counsel decides to call the witness anyway, many lawyers choose to "take the sting out" of the impeachment by eliciting the prior conviction themselves on direct examination, as a tactical matter. In *Ohler v. United States*, 529 U.S. 753 (2000), the U.S. Supreme Court held that a defendant whose own counsel introduced the impeaching conviction could not challenge the in limine ruling on appeal. Prior to *Ohler*, California courts permitted the in limine ruling to be challenged on appeal, and did not treat the anticipatory impeachment as a waiver. It remains to be seen whether the California Supreme Court will follow *Ohler* the same way it followed *Luce*.

10. CEC 1202, like FRE 806, permits hearsay declarants to be impeached to the same extent as if they actually testified in person. In *People v. Jacobs*, 78 Cal.App.4th 1444 (2000), a co-defendant sought admission of a pretrial admission by the defendant that he was the owner of the automobile where the stolen property was found. The defendant then demanded that the entire statement be admitted, pursuant to CEC 356. After its admission, the prosecution offered several of the defendant's prior felony convictions to impeach his hearsay statements. The Court upheld the impeachment under CEC 1202, even though the defendant did not personally testify at his trial. [**Examples: H-25, J-20**].

Chapter Sixteen

Review Materials for Character Evidence

All of the following twenty-two questions are based upon these facts:
Mr. and Mrs. Dee were divorced in 2002, and Mrs. Dee was awarded primary custody of Bradley, their two year old son. On June 12, 2003, Bradley was hospitalized with a fractured arm. Mrs. Dee told Dr. Good he fell out of a shopping cart. X-rays revealed several prior fractures, and that the spiral nature of the current fracture was inconsistent with a fall. Mrs. Neighbor, who has lived next door to Mrs. Dee for the past year, observed three occasions in early June, 2003, when Mrs. Dee hit Bradley with a stick around the head and arms because he did not respond quickly when called. As a result of these incidents, Mrs. Neighbor has a low opinion of Mrs. Dee, a judgment which is shared by most of the other neighbors, with the exception of Mrs. Friend, who is friendly with Mrs. Dee, has a good opinion of her, and considers her reputation to be good.

At each point where an objection is indicated in the following excerpts of testimony, assume an objection on the grounds of improper character evidence was asserted, and indicate by the appropriate letter if:

(a) The objection would be sustained and the answer would not be permitted whether the case were being tried in federal court or in a California state court;
(b) The objection would be overruled and the answer would be permitted whether the case were being tried in federal court or in a California state court;
(c) The objection would be sustained if the case were being tried in federal court, but overruled in a California state court;
(d) The objection would be overruled if the case were being tried in federal court, but sustained in a California state court.

The correct answers are found at the end of the questions.

Part A

Assume Mrs. Dee is prosecuted for criminal child abuse based on the fracture incident. During its case-in-chief, the prosecution calls Mrs. Neighbor, and the following questions are asked on direct examination.

Q. Are you acquainted with Mrs. Dee's reputation in the neighborhood regarding her fitness as a mother?
A. Yes.
Q. Please tell us what that reputation is?
1. Objection.
Q. Based upon your observations as a close neighbor, do you have an opinion concerning Mrs. Dee's fitness as a mother?
A. Yes.
Q. What is your opinion?
2. Objection.
Q. Have you ever observed Mrs. Dee beating her son, Bradley?
A. Yes.
Q. Please describe what you saw.
3. Objection.

Assume that during her defense, after her own testimony that Bradley fell out of a shopping cart, Mrs. Dee calls Mrs. Friend, who has known her and lived in the same neighborhood for two years, and the following questions are asked on direct examination:

Q. Are you acquainted with Mrs. Dee's reputation in the community regarding her fitness as a mother?
A. Yes.
Q. Please tell us what that reputation is?
4. Objection.
Q. Are you acquainted with Mrs. Dee's reputation in the community for use of force and violence?
A. Yes.
Q. Please tell us what that reputation is?
5. Objection.
Q. Are you acquainted with Mrs. Dee's reputation in the community for truthfulness?
A. Yes.
Q. Please tell us what that reputation is?
6. Objection.

Assuming Mrs. Friend were allowed to testify Mrs. Dee had a good reputation regarding her fitness as a mother, assume the prosecutor then asks the following questions on cross-examination:

Q. Mrs. Friend, have you heard that Mrs. Dee hit her son with a stick around the head and arms because he didn't respond quickly enough on three occasions in June of 2003?
7. Objection.
Q. Mrs. Friend, did you know that in May, 2003, Mrs. Dee was fired from her job as a waitress because she couldn't stay sober?
8. Objection.
Q. Mrs. Friend, have you heard that Mrs. Dee was convicted of assaulting a police officer in a bar-room brawl two years ago?
9. Objection.
Assuming Mrs. Friend were allowed to testify Mrs. Dee had a good reputation regarding her fitness as a mother, assume the prosecutor then recalls Mrs. Neighbor in rebuttal, and the following questions are asked:
Q. Based on your observations as a close neighbor, do you have an opinion concerning Mrs. Dee's fitness as a mother?
A. Yes.
Q. What is your opinion?
10. Objection.
Q. Are you acquainted with Mrs. Friend's reputation in the community for truthfulness?
A. Yes.
Q. Please tell us that that reputation is?
11. Objection.

Part B

Assume Mr. Dee brings suit to obtain custody of Bradley on the grounds Mrs. Dee is an unfit mother. He calls Mrs. Neighbor, and the following questions are asked on direct examination:
Q. Are you acquainted with Mrs. Dee's reputation in the neighborhood regarding her fitness as a mother?
A. Yes.
Q. Please tell us what that reputation is?
12. Objection.
Q. Based on your observations as a close neighbor, do you have an opinion concerning Mrs. Dee's fitness as a mother?
A. Yes.
Q. What is your opinion?
13. Objection.
Q. Have you ever observed Mrs. Dee beating her son, Bradley?
A. Yes.

Q. Please describe what you saw?
14. Objection.

Part C

Assume Mrs. Dee brings suit against an Insurer to recover on a policy covering accidental injury to any member of her family. The Insurer defends on the grounds the injuries were not accidental, but were intentionally inflicted by Mrs. Dee. After Mrs. Dee testifies that Bradley fell out of a shopping cart, she calls Mrs. Friend as a witness, and the following questions are asked on direct examination:

Q. Are you acquainted with Mrs. Dee's reputation in the neighborhood for peacefulness and non-violence?
A. Yes.
Q. Please tell us what that reputation is?
15. Objection.
Q. Do you have an opinion of Mrs. Dee's truthfulness?
A. Yes.
Q. Please tell us your opinion?
16. Objection.
Q. Does Mrs. Dee regularly attend the Foursquare Gospel Church every Sunday?
17. Objection.

Assume the Insurer then calls Mrs. Neighbor, and the following questions are asked on direct examination:

Q. Are you acquainted with Mrs. Dee's reputation in the neighborhood for use of force and violence?
A. Yes.
Q. Please tell us what that reputation is?
18. Objection.
Q. Are you acquainted with Mrs. Dee's reputation in the neighborhood for truthfulness?
A. Yes.
Q. Please tell us what that reputation is?
19. Objection.
Q. Based on your observations as a close neighbor, do you have an opinion concerning Mrs. Dee's propensity for the use of force and violence?
A. Yes.
Q. What is your opinion?
20. Objection.
Q. Based on your observations as a close neighbor, do you have an opinion concerning Mrs. Dee's truthfulness?

A. Yes.
Q. What is your opinion?
21. Objection.
Q. Have you ever observed Mrs. Dee beating her son Bradley?
A. Yes.
Q. Please describe what you observed?
22. Objection.

Answers to Review Questions on Character Evidence

1.(a). The only relevance is to show propensity, which is not permitted in the prosecution's case-in-chief.
2.(a). Same reason as 1.
3.(b). Admissible specific act to negate accident, CEC 1101(b) and FRE 404(b).
4.(b). Defendant can show *good* character to prove no propensity, CEC 1102, FRE 404(a).
5.(b). Same reason as 4; both traits are relevant.
6.(b). Same reason as 4; truthfulness is relevant to propensity; but (c) would be correct answer if reputation is offered to bolster her credibility as a witness; not admissible under FRE 608(a) since her credibility has not yet been challenged, but admissible under Prop. 8 in California.
7.(b). Proper cross-examination under *Michelson*.
8.(d). FRE 404 permits either form of question; CEC requires cross of reputation witness in form of "Have you heard?" rather than "Did you know?"
9.(a). Irrelevant to reputation of fitness as a mother.
10.(b). Bad reputation admissible to rebut evidence of good reputation, CEC 1102, FRE 404(a).
11.(b). Bad reputation admissible to attack credibility of witness, CEC 790, FRE 608(a).
12.(b). Character is directly in issue, CEC 1100, FRE 405(b).
13.(b). Same reason as 12.
14.(b). Same reason as 12.
15.(a). No propensity evidence allowed in civil suit, CEC 1101(a), FRE 404(a).
16.(a). Good reputation not admissible to bolster credibility except in rebuttal, CEC 790, FRE 608(a). Prop. 8 does not apply to civil case.
17.(a). Irrelevant, and note explicit exclusion in CEC 789 and FRE 610.
18.(a). Same reason as 15.
19.(b). Bad reputation admissible to attack her credibility as a witness, CEC 790, FRE 608(a).
20.(a). Same reason as 15.
21.(b). Same reason as 19.
22.(b). Admissible to negate accident rather than show propensity, CEC 1101(b), FRE 404(b).

Part IV

Competency and Personal Knowledge

Chapter Seventeen

Competency of Witnesses

Focus on CEC 700, 701, 702, 710 and 795

1. The disqualification of judges and jurors as witnesses is absolute under FRE 605 and 606. Under CEC 703 and 704, an objection to such testimony requires a mistrial, but the objection can be waived.
2. There is no general test of the competency of witnesses in the Federal Rules of Evidence, but CEC 701 requires both the capability to express oneself so as to be understood and the capability to understand the duty to tell the truth. Note that FRE 601 requires the federal courts to apply State law in determining the competency of a witness in civil actions, where State law supplies the rule of decision with respect to an element of a claim or defense.
3. The determination of the competency of a witness to testify is made by the court pursuant to CEC 405, while the determination of whether the witness has personal knowledge as required by CEC 702 is a question of conditional relevancy resolved pursuant to CEC 403. See the Law Revision Commission comment to CEC 701.
4. The issue of competency of witnesses arises most frequently when young children are called to testify. The judge has discretion to dispense with the oath for children under 10 who promise to tell the truth. CEC 710. It is error to preclude a child from testifying without conducting a *voir dire* examination to determine competency. *Bradburn v. Peacock*, 135 Cal.App.2d 161, 164–65 (1955). *In Re Crystal J.*, 218 Cal.App.3d 596, 601 (1990) upheld the disqualification of a 7 year old witness who stated he did not know the difference between the truth and a lie.

There are numerous California statutory provisions to accommodate the testimony of children. CEC 765(b) imposes a duty on the trial court of "special care" to protect witnesses under the age of 14. CEC 767(b) permits leading of child witnesses under the age of 10 in criminal prosecutions for child endangerment or lewd acts. California Penal Code §1346 permits video-taping of preliminary hearing testimony of a child under 16 for use at trial. California Penal Code §1347 permits two-way closed circuit television to be utilized for the testimony of children under 11. California Penal Code §868.5 permits the presence of a "support person" during a child's testimony.

5. Compare the determination of "competency" with the constitutional right to confront and cross examine the witnesses against you in a criminal trial. In *People v. White*, 238 N.E.2d 389 (Illinois Supreme Court, 1968), the witness was a patient in a nursing home whose ring was allegedly stolen by an orderly. Because of a stroke, the victim could only communicate by raising her right knee. She was instructed to raise her right knee if the answer to a question was "yes," and remain still if the answer was "no." When the defendant was brought in the room and she was asked if he stole her ring, she raised her knee. Try to formulate the questions that might be asked on cross examination to challenge the credibility of her identification of the defendant. Although she was a "competent" witness, the Illinois Supreme Court ruled that the defendant was deprived of his constitutional right to confront and cross examine. Compare the dissenting opinion of Judge John Noonan in *Walters v. McCormick*, 122 F.3d 1172 (9th Cir. 1997). A four year old child was finally deemed competent to testify after expressing great inconsistency and confusion about the meaning of "truth," when she said she would "tell the truth" because "you get a spanking" if you don't. Arguing that the judge and a psychologist "educated" her to give the responses they sought and to play "by their rules," Judge Noonan argued that the defendant was deprived of his constitutional right to cross-examine:

> Because she did not know what truth-telling is she was not a witness within the meaning of the Sixth Amendment. She could not be subjected to cross examination within the meaning of the Sixth Amendment. The purpose of cross examination is not only to test the accuracy of perception and the memory of the witness but to probe the witness' conscience, to discover whether in the story the witness is telling the witness is acting in accordance with the instruction of conscience to tell the truth. A witness who does not know what the truth is cannot be put to cross examination.

122 F.3d at 1182. Young children may have a tendency to give the answers which they believe the questioner wants to hear, resulting in inconsistency between their answers on direct examination and their answers on cross examination. Inconsistency, however, is treated as a question of credibility, not competency. *Adamson v. Dept. of Social Services*, 207 Cal.App.3d 14, 20 (1988).

6. We will encounter numerous hearsay exceptions which admit out of court statements by young children describing acts of child abuse. What if the child would not qualify as a competent witness in court? In the case of *In Re Cindy L.*, 17 Cal.4th 15 (1997), the California Supreme Court ruled that even though a three and one-half year old child was not competent to testify as a witness, her out of court statement could be admitted under a judicially crafted hearsay exception for alleged victims of child sexual abuse in juvenile court dependency hearings.

7. In *People v. Shirley*, 31 Cal.3d 18, 66–67 (1982), the California Supreme Court held that "the testimony of a witness who has undergone hypnosis for the purpose of restoring his memory of the events in issue is inadmissible as to all matters relating to those events, from the hypnotic session forward." The ruling exempted a criminal defendant's own testimony, however, to preserve his constitutional right to testify. Since this ruling excluded relevant evidence, it did not survive the enactment of Proposition 8 in criminal cases. The legislature then responded by enacting CEC 795, which was adopted by the required two-thirds margin. CEC 795 replaces the flat rule of exclusion announced in *Shirley* with a more limited exclusion. It permits testimony as to matters the witness recalled and related prior to the hypnosis, as long as procedural protections with regard to the conduct of the hypnosis are observed. In *People v. Aguilar*, 218 Cal.App.3d 1556 (1990), however, the Court held that the exception for the defendant's own testimony still applied, even though it was not referred to in CEC 795. Thus, the testimony of a criminal defendant subjected to hypnosis is never excluded. The testimony of other hypnotized witnesses in criminal cases will be admitted if there is compliance with CEC 795. The testimony of hypnotized witnesses in civil cases is still excluded by *Shirley*.

Chapter Eighteen

Personal Knowledge

Focus on CEC 702

1. "Personal knowledge" is defined in the Law Revision Commission Comment to CEC 702 as "a present recollection of an impression derived from the exercise of the witness' own senses." Compare CEC 170, defining "perceive."

2. Ordinarily, the personal knowledge of a witness is established by his or her own testimony, establishing he or she was present at the time an event or occurrence took place, and observed what happened. If there is evidence sufficient for the jury to find personal knowledge, the witness may then testify to his or her observations. Thus, personal knowledge is always a question of conditional relevance, decided pursuant to FRE 104(b) in federal court [See FRE 602], and CEC 403 in a California court. *Competency,* on the other hand, the capability to express oneself and understand the duty to tell the truth, is an issue decided by the judge pursuant to FRE 104(a) in federal court, and CEC 405 in a California court. Why the difference?

3. A trial judge generally has broad discretion to vary the order of proof, and permit evidence to be admitted provisionally, subject to a later offer of evidence proving a prerequisite preliminary fact. See CEC 320, 403(b). The CEC 702 requirement of personal knowledge is one of two exceptions in the California Evidence Code, where a party by objection can insist on proof of personal knowledge *before* the witness is allowed to testify concerning the matter. The other exception is CEC 720, relating to the qualification of experts. There are no similar exceptions under the Federal Rules of Evidence. [**Examples:** B-8, D-22, F-22, J-64, K-12].

4. Where personal knowledge is in dispute, how does a lawyer prove a witness is testifying based on personal knowledge? Consider the unusual case of George T. Franklin, who was convicted of murdering an eight-year-old girl twenty years earlier based on the testimony of his own daughter Eileen. She claimed that her memory of the grisly slaying had been "repressed" for twenty

years until it was dredged up during psychotherapy. The prosecution contended that her detailed account of the killing could only have been possible if she had actually been there. Eileen described her father crushing the skull of her playmate with a rock after he sexually assaulted her, vividly describing the crushing of a ring on the victim's finger as she held her hand over her head. When the body of the victim was recovered, the coroner concluded that her head had been crushed by a rock, and a crushed ring was found on the victim's finger.

The defense contended that the details in Eileen's account had been published in contemporary newspaper accounts of the murder. Eileen claimed she had never read them, and the defense was unable to prove that she had. The trial judge rejected evidence of the actual newspaper clippings, in the absence of evidence that Eileen had seen them. In closing argument, the prosecutor was permitted to argue that the details Eileen described could *only* have come from her actual presence at the scene of the murder.

In *Franklin v. Duncan*, 884 F.Supp. 1435 (N.D. Calif. 1995), *affirmed* 70 F.3d 75 (9th Cir. 1995), a federal court granted a writ of habeas corpus, invalidating Franklin's conviction after he had served five years of his sentence. Among the grounds relied upon by the court was the denial of due process by the erroneous exclusion of relevant, exculpatory evidence in the form of the news clippings:

> [P]etitioner Franklin was prevented from introducing evidence to disprove the contention that [Eileen's] memory of minute details of the crime scene could only be attributable to petitioner's commission of the offense. The newspaper articles disprove the contention that [Eileen] must have witnessed the murder, as there was no other way she could have known the details of the crime. As petitioner's counsel posed the issue at oral argument:
> It occurred to me this morning that were I to be arrested and charged in Oakland with committing a crime yesterday, and were my alibi to be, I was not in Oakland yesterday, I could not have committed the crime, I was standing in front of the White House, and I can prove I was standing in front of the White House because I can describe an extraordinary event that happened there, I can tell you that the police shot a man, I can tell you what he was wearing, I can tell you that there was a knife taped to his wrist...and there's no way that I would know all these facts which are true were I not at the White House. I submit to you that the proposition that the prosecution in that situation could not admit the Chronicle this morning which contains the picture and contains every detail I'm talking about [is ludicrous]....

That fact would come in like a hot knife through butter.... Respondent argues that [the newspaper clippings were] not admissible because petitioner did not lay a proper foundation by proving that [Eileen] had read any of the newspaper articles. Such a "foundation" is not required. In the above hypothetical, the government would not be required to first prove that the defendant had read the Chronicle article about the White House shooting in order to introduce the article. [The newspaper clipping] was being proffered to disprove the prosecution's contention that [Eileen's] repressed memory must have been correct, because there was no other way [Eileen] could have known the details of the crime. As such, it was directly and critically relevant to the defense. Consequently, "the evidence should have been admitted as constitutionally required to protect [petitioner's] rights under the Confrontation Clause." *United States v. Begay*, 937 F.2d 515, 523 n.19 (10th Cir. 1991).

Franklin's subsequent efforts to recover damages against his daughter, her psychotherapist and the investigating police officers were rejected. *Franklin v. Ter*, 201 F.3d 1098 (9th Cir. 2000); *Franklin v. Fox*, 312 F.3d 423 (9th Cir. 2002). In the civil cases, evidence was presented that Eileen's former husband hated Franklin and was obsessed with the earlier murder case, compiling a large file of newspaper clippings.

Part V

The Hearsay Rule and Its Exceptions

Chapter Nineteen

Hearsay Defined

Focus on CEC 225, 1200

1. There is no essential difference between the definitions of hearsay in the Federal Rules of Evidence and the California Evidence Code. While the FRE uses the term "assertion" in defining a "statement," and the CEC uses the term "expression," the words are synonymous.

2. The hearsay rule excludes relevant evidence, but Section 28(d) of Proposition 8 provides an explicit exception for "any existing statutory rule of evidence relating to hearsay." New hearsay exceptions have been created since the enactment of Proposition 8 in 1982, but we need not check to see if they were enacted by a two-thirds vote: *exceptions* to the hearsay rule do not *exclude* relevant evidence—they permit its admission. Would the repeal or abolition of a hearsay exception in California require a two-thirds vote to apply in criminal cases?

3. Note the semantic difference between the FRE and the CEC in the treatment of prior statements of a witness and admissions of a party. FRE provides that they are "not hearsay," while the California Evidence Code treats them as "exceptions" to the hearsay rule. The result is the same: they can be admitted in evidence.

4. When a statement is not offered to prove the truth of what is asserted, but for some other *relevant* purpose, it will be admitted and a limiting instruction can be requested.

There are three frequently recurring situations where out of court statements are often admitted to prove something other than the truth of what is asserted:

First, when the making of the statement itself has some operative legal effect, such as the words of agreement to a contract, or the words that allegedly libeled the plaintiff.
[Example: A-5].

Second, when the fact that the declarant stated the words proves his knowledge of what was stated, or otherwise itself demonstrates his state of mind. [**Examples: B-45, E-30, E-43, F-17, J-87, K-3, K-4, K-31, K-65, L-8, L-20**]. The manner in which the words were spoken may also be relevant to show the condition of the declarant, such as slurred speech. [**Example: J-9**]. The very fact that the declarant spoke, without regard to the truth of what he said, could be offered to prove he was alive at the time the statement was made. [**Example: K-3**].

Third, the fact that the words were said in the listener's presence could prove the listener's knowledge of what was stated, or explain his subsequent conduct. [**Examples: A-13, B-31, C-32, D-10, E-26, F-4, G-4, G-40, H-3, H-9, H-15, H-27, H-31, H-47, J-3, K-18, L-4, L-22, L-94**].

Under all three of these circumstances, the credibility of the declarant is not at issue, so there is no need for cross-examination. The issue presented is simply whether the statement was made or not. As to that issue, the credibility of the witness testifying in court that the statement was, in fact, made can be tested by cross-examination.

5. If silence is intended to communicate an assertion, the silence itself may be hearsay. A shrug or vacant stare in response to a pointed question is ordinarily treated as an intended assertion, and may be admitted under the exception to the hearsay rule for admissions of a party. But if evidence that something was not said is offered to show it didn't happen, because something would have been said if it did happen, the evidence is not hearsay because no assertion was intended. [**Examples: C-17, D-31, E-28, G-10, H-38, H-43, J-35**].

Chapter Twenty

Party Admissions

Focus on CEC 1220–1224

1. The CEC 1220 exception for party admissions is identical to FRE 801(d)(2)(A). Note that both refer to the statement as an "admission." Don't get confused by the ordinary meaning of "admission" as a concession of fault or liability. The statement of a party, when offered against him, always comes within the exception as long as it is relevant; it need not "admit" anything. In fact, it may be a denial or explanation which the offering party intends to prove was false or misleading. [Examples: A-5, B-8, C-20, C-35, E-28, E-34, F-4, F-13, F-17, G-42, G-52, G-55, H-51, K-10, K-39, K-48, K-114, L-6, L-10, L-20].

There is *another* hearsay exception, which we will consider later, for a statement which was against the declarant's self-interest at the time it was made. CEC 1230. That exception can only be used if the declarant is unavailable, however, so it could not be used against a party. But you wouldn't need it to admit a party's statement. Under CEC 1220 and FRE 801(d)(2)(A), the party's statement will be admissible even if it was fully self-serving, and not against his self-interest at the time it was made.

A party cannot offer his own out of court statements, but CEC 356 may present an opportunity to have exculpatory out-of-court statements admitted when the opposing party offers only an incriminating *portion* of the statement. In *People v. O.J. Simpson*, the prosecution decided not to offer the lengthy exculpatory statement Simpson made to the police after his arrest. The defense, of course, would have loved to have the jury hear Simpson's explanations without subjecting him to cross examination, but the hearsay rule would exclude it, and the CEC 1220 exception was only available to the prosecution. When a prosecution expert testified that he was surprised that his forensic testing implicated Simpson, because he had heard on the news that Simpson had an "airtight alibi," the defense argued that Simpson's entire statement should come in under CEC 356. Judge Ito ruled that the expert's testimony did not open the door" to allow admission of the complete statement, and the jury in the criminal trial never heard the contents of the police interview of Simpson. In the civil trial, where Simpson was called to testify by the plaintiffs, the statement was used in cross examination to show prior inconsistencies. [Examples: F-19, H-71].

If the defense *succeeds* in getting exculpatory statements admitted under CEC 356, it may be a hollow victory. The statements can then be impeached to the same extent as if the defendant testified, under CEC 1202. In *People v. Jacobs*, 78 Cal.App.4th 1444 (2000), the court held that the defendant's prior convictions were admissible to impeach his exculpatory statements admitted pursuant to CEC 356, even though he never testified at his trial.

2. The CEC 1221 exception for "adoptive" admissions is identical to FRE 801(d)(2)(B). Where there is some ambiguity as to whether the words or other conduct of a party "manifested his adoption or his belief in [the] truth" of a statement, the statement will be admitted upon introduction of evidence "sufficient to sustain a finding" of that fact, and the question will be determined by the fact-finder pursuant to CEC 403.

3. The CEC 1222 exception for "authorized" admissions differs from FRE 801(d)(2)C) in several important respects. First, FRE 801(d)(2)(C) includes statements made by an authorized agent to anyone, including the principal himself. CEC 1222 only extends to situations where the agent is speaking "for" the principal to third persons. See Advisory Committee's Note, FRE 801(d)(2)(C). [Example: A-11]. Second, FRE 801(d)(2)(C) does not extend to situations of "apparent" authority, where the statement is not expressly authorized, but is still made within the "scope" of the agent's employment. Such statements are treated separately by FRE 801(d)(2)(D). The California Evidence Code does not have an exception equivalent to 801(d)(2)(D), however. Nonetheless, "apparent" authority may be brought within CEC 1222 by relying upon the Law Revision Commission Comment to CEC 1222, which states that "[t]he authority of the declarant to make the statement need not be express, it may be implied. It is to be determined in each case under the substantive law of agency." In *W.T. Grant Co. v. Superior Court*, 23 Cal.App.3d 284 (1972), the statement of a company manager that selling used TV's as new was "company policy" was admitted because he was "acting within the scope of his employment" when he made the statement. The third difference between FRE 801(d)(2)(C) and CEC 1222 relates to how the preliminary fact of authority is established. Under CEC 1222, it is treated as a CEC 403 issue of conditional relevancy. The statement itself cannot be used to establish that it is authorized, since the proponent must first offer admissible evidence sufficient to sus-

tain a finding of the requisite authority. See CEC 1222(b). Under FRE 801(d)(2)(C), however, the issue of authority will be resolved by the judge pursuant to FRE 104(a). The statement itself *can* be considered, although the 1997 amendment to FRE 801(d)(2) provides the statement "alone" is not sufficient to establish the authority. [**Example: B-26**].

4. There is no California equivalent to FRE 801(d)(2)(D), but the same result can often be achieved by arguing that authority can be implied under CEC 1222. California also permits admission of an agent's statement where the liability of the party against whom the statement is offered is based upon vicarious liability for the conduct of the agent. CEC 1224. This exception is only available in civil cases, however. In *Labis v. Stopper,* 11 Cal.App.3d 1003 (1970), for example, a painting contractor was sued for injuries the plaintiff received when one of his employees moved a drop cloth while she was walking on it. The employee told an investigating police officer that he "was not aware that anyone was on the drop cloth" when he moved it. The statement was not "authorized," nor was it within the scope of the employee's employment, but it was admitted against the contractor under CEC 1224, because his liability was based upon the liability of the employee. [**Examples: H-7, H-27, H-36, J-33**].

5. The CEC 1223 exception for co-conspirator's statements is comparable to FRE 801(d)(2)(E). The California exception appears slightly broader, since it explicitly encompasses statements made prior to the party's participation in the conspiracy, while FRE 801(d)(2)(E) appears to only include statements made "during the course" of the party's participation in the conspiracy. However, the Supreme Court construed the co-conspirator exception to include even statements made prior to the time a party joined the conspiracy prior to the enactment of the Federal Rules. *United States v. United States Gypsum Co.,* 333 U.S. 364 (1948). More important, the preliminary facts of the existence of the conspiracy and the membership of both the declarant and the party against whom the statement is offered must be independently established by admissible evidence sufficient to sustain a finding under CEC 403 and 1223(c). Under FRE 801(d)(2)(E), and the decision of the U.S. Supreme Court in *Bourjaily v. United States,* 483 U.S. 171 (1987), these preliminary facts will be determined by the judge under FRE 104(a), and the judge can consider the statement itself in determining them. The 1997 amendment to FRE 801(d)(2), however, provides the statement alone will not be sufficient to establish the preliminary facts. [**Examples: A-11, A-21**].

Chapter Twenty-One

Prior Statements of a Witness

Focus on CEC 770, 791, 1235, 1236, 1238

1. When a prior inconsistency is offered to "impeach" a witness, *i.e.*, to attack the credibility of his present testimony in court because he said something different on a prior occasion, we don't need a hearsay exception. The prior statement is not offered to prove the truth of what was asserted; just the making of the statement, whether it is true or not, establishes the inconsistency that makes the witness less credible. Under CEC 770 and FRE 613(b), however, the examiner must first give the witness an opportunity to explain or deny the statement. If he *admits* making the statement, no "extrinsic" proof of the statement is necessary. If he *denies* making the statement, the examiner can then offer "extrinsic" evidence that the statement was in fact made. Ordinarily, "extrinsic" evidence consists of a witness like a police officer, who testifies he was present and heard the witness make the inconsistent statement. Lawyers who interview hostile witnesses need to be careful they don't find themselves in the position of being the only person who can testify that the witness said something inconsistent with their present testimony in a pretrial interview, since ethical rules preclude a lawyer from being an advocate and a witness in the same trial.

The examiner need not show the inconsistent statement to the witness before asking him about it, although the statement should be shown to opposing counsel. CEC 769, FRE 613(a). Simply ask the witness if he spoke with X on such and such a date, and whether he said to X the words you contend are inconsistent with his present testimony. If the witness denies it, the impeachment is completed by calling X during your case, and having him testify that the witness spoke the quoted words to him. [**Examples:** A-29, A-45, J-33, J-92, K-15, K-33, K-114, L-26].

2. Does CEC 770 exclude relevant evidence? In a criminal case, could a lawyer insist that extrinsic evidence of a prior inconsistent statement is admissible even when the witness was never confronted with it, because of Proposition 8? If so, could the trial judge exclude it under CEC 352? If the prior inconsistent statement is offered to impeach a hearsay statement admitted under an exception to the hearsay rule, CEC 770 need not be complied with. CEC 1202.

3. When the prior inconsistency is offered "substantively," *i.e.*, to prove the truth of what is asserted, FRE 801(d)(1)(A) requires that the statement have been given under oath at a trial, hearing or other proceeding. CEC 1235, however, does *not* require that the inconsistent statement have been under oath. As long as the statement is inconsistent with the present testimony, and is offered in compliance with CEC 770, it comes in to prove the truth of what was asserted. This difference between the Federal and California rule can determine the outcome of a case. Assume, for example, the defendant is on trial for a burglary in which a unique diamond ring was stolen. The stolen ring is located in a pawn shop. The pawn shop operator tells a police officer that he is certain the ring was pawned by the defendant one day after the burglary took place. At the trial, however, the pawn shop operator testifies that he is "not sure" when the ring was pawned or who pawned it. Under FRE 801(d)(1)(A), the prior statement to the police officer cannot be admitted to prove the truth of what was asserted, since it was not given under oath. It could only be offered to challenge the credibility of the pawn shop owner's testimony that he was "not sure." Under CEC 1235, however, the prior statement to the police officer would be admitted to prove that the defendant pawned the ring the day after the burglary. If believed by the jury, it would even be sufficient to convict the defendant of the burglary. In *California v. Green*, 399 U.S. 149 (1970), the U.S. Supreme Court ruled that the California hearsay exception for prior inconsistent statements did not violate the defendant's constitutional right to confront and cross-examine the witnesses against him.

4. If a witness simply answers "I don't remember," does a prior statement in which he recounted the requested information qualify as a "prior inconsistent statement"? If the loss of memory is genuine and total, the prior statement is not inconsistent and would not be admissible to impeach. *People v. Sam*, 71 Cal.2d 194 (1969). If the lapse of memory is partial or selective, or total but evasive or contrived, the impeachment will be permitted. The judge will determine the *bona fide* of the memory lapse pursuant to CEC 405. If the witness claims to have no memory of making the prior inconsistent statement, it can be proved extrinsically, since the witness was given the *opportunity* to explain or deny it. CEC 770. [**Example: C-39**].

5. A prior *consistent* statement is admissible to "rehabilitate" a witness who has been impeached, either by a prior inconsistent statement or by an express or implied charge that his testimony was recently fabricated or influenced by bias or improper motive. But the consistent statement must have been made *before* the inconsistent statement, or before the bias, motive for fabrication or other improper motive arose. CEC 791. While FRE 801(d)(1)(B) does not explicitly require that the consistent statement precede the motive for fabrication, this requirement was imposed in *Tome v. United States,* 513 U.S. 150 (1995). Nor does FRE 801(d)(1)(B) explicitly refer to use of a prior inconsistency as an alternative prerequisite to offering a prior consistency, but federal courts generally treat impeachment by prior inconsistency as an implied charge of recent fabrication and permit the prior consistency to be shown. When a prior consistency is admitted, it comes in both to bolster the credibility of the in-court testimony, and to prove the truth of what is asserted, whether it was under oath or not. FRE 801(d)(1)(B); CEC 1236. [**Examples:** C-25, L-24, L-28, L-36, L-56, L-58].

The use of prior consistency is well illustrated by *People v. Cannaday,* 8 Cal.3d 379 (1972). The defendant, a prison inmate, was on trial for assaulting a fellow prisoner by striking him with a baseball bat. The witness, another inmate, testified he saw the defendant strike the victim with the bat. On cross-examination, the witness was impeached with a statement to a prison guard right after the incident, that he "didn't see anything." He was also asked whether the prosecutor told him the day before he testified that "the judge can rehear your case after you testify." The prosecution then offered a lengthy interview statement several weeks after the incident, which was consistent with the witness' trial testimony. The court held that while the consistent statement was not admissible under CEC 791(a), because it was *after* the inconsistent statement, it could still be admitted under CEC 791(b). The court reasoned that the statement preceded the implied charge of bias arising from the prosecutor's promise of a potential reward for his testimony by having his own case reheard.

6. Does CEC 791 exclude relevant evidence? Could a lawyer in a criminal case bolster a witness' credibility by eliciting prior consistent statements before the witness is even cross-examined, arguing that CEC 791 is abrogated in criminal cases by Proposition 8? Could a judge exclude the prior consistent statements under CEC 352, because it has slight probative value in the absence of a challenge to the witness' credibility, and would require undue consumption of time?

7. The FRE 801(d)(1)(C) exception for statements of identification permits prior identifications that may be inconsistent with present testimony to be admitted to prove the truth of what was asserted, even if the statement was not under oath. It also permits extrinsic proof of the prior identification without

compliance with FRE 613(b), and permits prior consistent identifications to be admitted without a previous challenge to the credibility of the witness. CEC 1238 is much narrower in its application, since the witness must testify that he made the identification and that it was a true reflection of his opinion at that time. CEC 1238(c). [**Example: D-16**]. But if the witness denies having made the prior identification, or says it wasn't true, the prior identification can be offered as a prior inconsistent statement under CEC 1235. Doesn't that render the protection of CEC 1238(c) illusory?

8. The facts of *People v. Chavez*, 26 Cal.3d 334 (1980) neatly illustrate the differences between the Federal Rules of Evidence and the California Evidence Code with respect to the prior statements of witnesses. A hostile encounter between two Los Angeles street gangs led to a drive-by shooting. "Angel" was in the crowd of young men who ducked for cover when the shooting started. He was called as a witness at the defendant's trial, and asked if he saw who fired the shots from the passing car. He answered, "No."

The prosecutor then elicited the following prior statements:

(a) Two days after the incident, Angel told a police officer that "Bird fired the shots."

["Bird" was the street name used by the defendant].

(b) Several weeks later, Angel was interviewed by another police officer, and signed a written statement which said, "[Bird] had a rifle. He pointed it out the window and fired once."

(c) Angel was called as a witness at the preliminary hearing, and in response to a question from the judge, "Did you see the defendant fire a gun at the crowd," he responded, "Yes."

Would the first and second statements be admissible to prove that Bird fired the gun under CEC 1235? Under CEC 1238?

If the case were being tried in federal court, because the shooting took place on federal property, would the first and second statements be admissible to prove Bird fired the gun under FRE 801(d)(1)(A)? Under FRE 801(d)(1)(C)? Would your answer be the same for the preliminary hearing testimony? Why not?

CHAPTER TWENTY-TWO

Past Recollection Recorded and Recollection Refreshed

Focus on CEC 771, 1237

1. Anything can be used to "refresh" a witness' recollection, whether it was prepared by the witness or not. Refreshing recollection and past recollection recorded are often treated together because these devices are frequently used in tandem by trial lawyers: if a writing does *not* refresh the witness' recollection, an attempt will then be made to enter the writing in evidence under the hearsay exception for past recollection recorded. Recall that a claimed loss of memory may be challenged by offering a prior statement as an inconsistent statement, and under CEC 1235 it will be admitted to prove the truth of what is asserted. Here, however, we deal with a genuine loss of memory, by first seeking to refresh and restore it, and if that fails, by offering the next best thing, a writing made when the memory was fresh.

2. CEC 771 is very similar to FRE 612, insofar as both give the adverse party a right to inspect the writing used to refresh recollection, and use it to cross examine the witness. Portions of it may even be offered in evidence. It might contain inconsistencies with the testimony in court, for example, or reveal a bias. Unlike FRE 612, however, CEC 771 makes no distinction between writings used while testifying and those used prior to testifying. FRE 612 gives the judge greater discretion to limit production in the latter case. And unlike FRE 612, CEC 771 mandates striking the testimony if the writing is not produced. Under FRE 612, the judge is given greater leeway to fashion a remedy; striking the testimony is only mandated when the prosecution refuses to produce the writing in a criminal case. [**Example: B-53**].

3. The hearsay exception for past recollection recorded contained in CEC 1237 is very similar to FRE 803(5). Both require that the witness now have insufficient present recollection to testify fully and accurately, and both require that the writing have been made when the matter was fresh in the witness' memory. FRE 803(5), however, requires that the statement have been "made or adopted" by the witness. CEC 1237(a)(2)(ii) allows a statement made by some other person for the purpose of recording the witness' statement at the time it was made. Thus, the statement of a witness to a police officer recorded in a police report would be inadmissible under FRE 803(5), if the report had never been shown to the witness and "adopted." It could be admitted under CEC 1237, however, if the witness now testifies his statement was true, and it is authenticated as an accurate record.

4. Under both CEC 1237 and FRE 803(5), if the past recollection recorded is admitted, it can only be read to the jury, so it will not be given greater weight than other oral testimony. The adverse party, however, may offer the writing in evidence. When might he wish to do so?

CHAPTER TWENTY-THREE

SPONTANEOUS AND CONTEMPORANEOUS STATEMENTS, AND STATEMENTS OF PHYSICAL OR MENTAL CONDITION

Focus on CEC 1240, 1241, 1251, 1253 and 1260

1. While CEC 1240 appears similar to the FRE 803(2) exception for "excited utterance," note that CEC 1240 requires the declarant *perceive* the exciting event, act or condition, and the statement must purport to "narrate, describe or explain" what was perceived. [**Examples: F-7, G-52, H-18, J-46, J-52, L-4**]. FRE 803(2), on the other hand, only requires that the statement "relate" to a startling event while under the stress of excitement caused by the event. The difference can be illustrated by the following hypothetical. The mother of a ten year old girl receives a telephone call informing her that her daughter has been murdered. She screams, "Oh, my God, I never should have let George take her!" George is now on trial for kidnapping and murder. He claims the death was accidental, but may face a murder conviction based on a felony murder theory if he is convicted of kidnapping. He wants to offer the mother's statement to defend against the kidnapping charge, to show the mother consented to his taking of the child. FRE 803(2) would clearly allow the statement to be admitted; the startling event is the death of the daughter, and the statement was under the stress of excitement caused by the death. FRE 803(2) does not require the declarant to have actually perceived the startling event. Under CEC 1240, one might argue that the "event" perceived was the telephone call

informing her of her daughter's death, but the statement does not purport to narrate, describe or explain the phone call. [**Examples: A-23, E-26**].

2. CEC 1241 requires that a contemporaneous statement explain, qualify or make understandable *conduct* in which the declarant was engaged. FRE 803(1), on the other hand, only requires the declarant to *perceive* the event or condition which is described or explained. Thus, the automobile passenger who says, "Boy, that yellow car is sure going fast," would easily fall within FRE 803(1), and might even come within FRE 803(2) if excited. CEC 1241 would not apply, however, since the statement does not explain "conduct" of the passenger. The only way to get the statement admitted is to show "excitement" under CEC 1240.

3. Can the statement itself be offered to show the requisite "excitement," or would this be impermissible "boot-strapping"? If excitement is to be *inferred* from the tone of voice and manner of speech, then the statement is not being offered to prove the truth of what is asserted, and would not be hearsay. Thus, even under the California Evidence Code, the statement itself could show the "excitement" that then qualifies it to be admitted to prove the truth of what is asserted under the CEC 1240 hearsay exception. Would the requisite showing of "excitement" be a CEC 403 question for the jury, or a CEC 405 question for the judge?

4. The closest parallel to FRE 803(3) in the California Evidence Code is CEC 1250. CEC 1250(a)(2) makes explicit the implicit limitation of FRE 803(3) noted in the Report of the House Committee on the Judiciary: when offered to prove conduct in conformity with the expressed intent, as in *Mutual Life Ins. Co. v. Hillmon*, 145 U.S. 285 (1892), the evidence can only be offered to prove the future conduct of the declarant, not the future conduct of another person. Where a statement of intent implicates the plans of others, it may be difficult for a jury to consider the evidence only to show the conduct of the declarant. In *People v. Alcalde*, 24 Cal.2d 177 (1944), for example, the victim of a murder said she was "going out with Frank" the evening she was murdered. The statement was admitted against the defendant, whose name was Frank, to prove he murdered the victim that evening. The California Supreme Court upheld the conviction, noting that the jury had been instructed that the evidence "was admitted for the limited purpose of showing the decedent's intention." Why is the decedent's intention relevant, except to identify Frank as the person she was with when she was murdered? Whether the subsequent enactment of CEC 1250(a)(2) limits or overrules the *Alcalde* decision remains an open question in California. *See People v. Melton*, 44 Cal.3d 713, 739 (1988). [**Examples: A-23, G-4, G-32, J-1, J-3, J-9, L-8, L-18**].

5. If the declarant's state of mind is itself in issue, CEC 1250(a)(1) allows the statement to prove the state of mind. For example, the declarant's statement,

"I am really feeling so depressed I don't want to go on living," would be admissible to show the declarant's state of depression. [**Example: H-21**]. CEC 1251 carries this theory of admissibility a step beyond FRE 803(3), by allowing a statement of memory or belief of a *prior* state of mind which is itself an issue in the action. For example, the statement "I felt so confused the week after my husband died that I really didn't understand anything I was doing," would be admissible under CEC 1251 to prove the declarant was confused when she signed a contract, but not under FRE 803(3). CEC 1251 requires that the declarant be unavailable, however.

6. Just as FRE 803(3) makes an exception to the inadmissibility of statements of memory or belief for statements related to the execution, revocation, identification or terms of the declarant's will, the California Evidence Code carves out a similar exception in CEC 1260. Unlike FRE 803(3), however, the California exception requires the unavailability of the declarant.

7. There is no broad exception for "medical diagnosis" under the California Evidence Code, as there is in FRE 803(4). CEC 1253 is only available for minor victims of child abuse. CEC 1250 and 1251, however, create broad exceptions for statements describing "mental feeling, pain or bodily health" that might be made to a physician for purpose of diagnosis. Neither exception requires that medical diagnosis or treatment be the purpose of the statement, however. Unlike FRE 803(4), these exceptions would not extend to statements describing "the inception or general character of the cause or external source" of the symptoms. [**Examples: D-14, L-36, L-44**].

v

Chapter Twenty-Four

Business and Official Records Exceptions

Focus on CEC 1270, 1271, 1280, 1560–62

1. The CEC 1271 hearsay exception for business records is generally the same as FRE 803(6). "Business" is defined even more broadly in CEC 1270 than in FRE 803(6), to include governmental activity. Unlike FRE 803(6), however, CEC 1271 does not explicitly include "opinions, or diagnoses." While opinions in business records are not necessarily excluded, the California courts take a more restrictive approach, limiting opinions to readily observable acts, events or conditions. *People v. Reyes,* 12 Cal.3d 486, 502–504 (1974). A more complex opinion, such as a psychiatric diagnosis, will be excluded. *People v. Campos,* 32 Cal.4th 304, 307–308 (1995). [**Example: L-24**].

2. The comment to CEC 1271 makes it clear that police accident and arrest reports cannot be admitted to show observations or accounts of persons who have no business duty to report to the police. Where police officers have a duty to report to the reporting officer, however, their statements will be admissible. [**Example: J-56**].

3. The CEC 1280 hearsay exception for records by public employees is duplicative of the CEC 1271 business records exception, which also applies to governmental records. But CEC 1280 does not require a witness to testify to the identity of the record and its mode of preparation, as does CEC 1271. This allows the court to take judicial notice of circumstances assuring the trustworthiness of the records.

4. Unlike FRE 803(8), the California Evidence Code has no explicit exclusion in criminal cases for matters observed by law enforcement personnel. In *United States v. Oates,* 560 F.2d 45 (2nd Cir. 1977), the court applied the FRE 803(8) exclusion to 803(6) as well, holding that a chemist's identification of illicit drugs could not be proven by offering his official report as a business

record. Presented with the same circumstances, California courts have ruled that the identification of drugs by a laboratory analyst could be established by offering his report as an official record under CEC 1280. *People v. Parker,* 8 Cal.App.4th 110 (1992). [**Example: E-18**]. But a laboratory report may be a "testimonial" statement encompassed by the constitutional right of confrontation recognized in *Crawford v. Washington, infra* p. 107. *Compare State v. Williams,* 644 N.W.2d 919 (Wis. 2002) *with Commonwealth v. Verde,* 827 N.E.2d 701 (Mass. 2005).

5. Both CEC 1271 and 1280 require that the writing be "contemporaneous," *i.e.,* "made at or near the time of the act, condition or event." In *People v. Martinez,* 22 Cal.4th 106 (2000), the California Supreme Court held that printouts from a computer database maintained by the State Department of Justice could be admitted under CEC 1280 to prove prior felony convictions charged as enhancements against the defendant. Although no evidence was offered that entries in the computer database were made at or near the time of the felony conviction, the court relied on statutes requiring the reporting of convictions in a timely manner, and applied the evidentiary presumption in CEC 664 that official duty has been regularly performed.

6. Just as in FRE 803(7) and 803(10), the California Evidence Code provides a hearsay exception for the *absence* of entry in a business record, CEC 1272, or official record, CEC 1284. These exceptions are no more necessary than are the federal exceptions, since the absence of a record would not be hearsay anyway, since it is not an intended assertion. [**Example: D-12**].

7. CEC 1560-62 provide that routine business records can be offered in evidence without requiring the actual appearance of the custodian of records. The records must be accompanied by an affidavit establishing the requisite foundational requirements. An amendment to the FRE adopted in 2000 now permits a similar procedure to be followed in federal courts. See FRE 902(11) and 902(12).

Chapter Twenty-Five

Unavailability Exceptions

Focus on CEC 240, 1242, 1230 and 1350

1. Under the Federal Rules of Evidence, the hearsay exceptions that require a preliminary showing of the unavailability of the declarant are conveniently grouped in FRE 804. In the California Evidence Code, however, they are scattered throughout the Code. The California unavailability exceptions include exceptions that parallel all five of the exceptions in FRE 804: former testimony [CEC 1290–92] (separately covered in Chapter Twenty-six, *infra*); dying declarations [CEC 1242]; declarations against interest [CEC 1230]; statements of family history [CEC 1310, 1311]; and a narrower version of forfeiture by wrongdoing, limited to criminal cases [CEC 1350]. But there are other California exceptions that also require a showing of unavailability, including two we have already examined: the statement of previously existing mental or physical state [CEC 1251], and the statement regarding a will [CEC 1260]. In this chapter, after examining the meaning of "unavailable," we will consider the dying declaration, the declaration against interest, and forfeiture by wrongdoing.

2. The preliminary showing of unavailability is *not* a question of conditional relevance; it is decided by the judge pursuant to CEC 405. The proponent of a hearsay declaration has the burden of proving the unavailability of the declarant as a witness by a preponderance of the evidence.

3. The circumstances that establish "unavailability" are laid out in CEC 240, which generally track the circumstances laid out in FRE 804(a). There is one important difference. CEC 240 does *not* include a witness who contemptuously persists in refusing to testify despite an order of the court to do so, as in FRE 804(a)(2). In *People v. Rojas*, 13 Cal.3d 540 (1975), the court ruled that a young man who witnessed a gang killing and testified at a preliminary hearing, but later refused to testify at trial despite a grant of immunity, was "unavailable" because of "mental illness or infirmity" under CEC 240(a)(3), since he was motivated by fear for his personal safety and that of his family. Thus,

his preliminary hearing testimony was admissible under the former testimony exception in CEC 1291. The *Rojas* reasoning would not apply, however, to a witness whose refusal to testify was motivated by considerations other than fear. What if it was motivated by personal loyalty? [**Example: G-31**].

4. Under both FRE 804(a) and CEC 240(b), if the proponent of the hearsay statement procured the unavailability of the declarant, or engaged in wrongdoing to prevent the declarant from testifying, the showing of unavailability will be defeated and the hearsay exception will not be available. The party objecting to the evidence has the burden of proving that the unavailability of the declarant was procured by the proponent. *See* Comment to CEC 405. In *People v. Rojas, supra,* the court noted that the threats and conduct that made the witness fearful came from persons other than the proponent of his former testimony, *i.e.,* the prosecution. If the prosecution were able to prove that the defendant was the source of the threats, it could have utilized the exception in CEC 1350, which is even broader than the former testimony exception. It requires only that the prior statement be memorialized in a tape recording or in a notarized written statement.

5. The exception for the "dying declaration" in FRE 804(b)(2) is limited to civil actions and homicide prosecutions. There is no such limitation in CEC 1242. The Comment to CEC 1242 suggests that there is "no rational basis" for the distinction made in FRE 804(b)(2) between homicide cases and other crimes. Nor does CEC 1242 explicitly require unavailability of the declarant, although he would not be a "dying person" unless he subsequently died. FRE 804(b)(2) could be used to admit a statement made in contemplation of death by a person who recovered and later became unavailable for some other reason. It does not appear that CEC 1242 could be used in this manner, since one who recovered would not be a "dying person." [**Examples: D-14, D-16**]. Nor would one contemplating suicide be a "dying person." [**Example: H-21**]. If CEC 1242 were construed to only require that the declarant believed his death was imminent, as in FRE 804(b)(2), then it would no longer be an "unavailability" exception. CEC 1242 requires *both* that the declarant be a "dying person," and that he speak "under a sense of immediately pending death." [**Example: J-46**]. Finally, note that CEC 1242 explicitly requires that the dying declarant's statement be made upon personal knowledge. Thus, the statement of a man choking to death at the dinner table proclaiming that "my wife poisoned me," or the statement of a man shot in the back identifying the person who shot him may not be admissible unless there is evidence sufficient to support a finding that the dying declarant had personal knowledge of the cause of his death. [**Example: F-7**]. While there is no explicit requirement of personal knowledge in any of the federal hearsay exceptions, the introduction to the Advisory

Committee's Notes for both Rules 803 and 804 indicate "firsthand knowledge" is a prerequisite for admission, which may appear from the statement or be inferable from the circumstances.

6. The hearsay exception for the statement against interest in CEC 1230 is somewhat broader than FRE 804(b)(3), since it includes statements which create a risk of making the declarant "an object of hatred, ridicule or social disgrace in the community." Consider, for example, the corporate manager who is accused of sexual harassment for pressuring a subordinate employee into an illicit affair. Confronted with her accusation of sexual harassment, he admits the affair but says it was "voluntary," then commits suicide. In a suit against the corporation, would his statement admitting the affair be admissible? Could it qualify as an agent's admission? As a dying declaration? As a declaration against interest? Would the ruling on admissibility in federal court be different than the ruling under the California Evidence Code? [**Examples: H-7, H-36**].

7. Where a declaration against interest is offered to exculpate a criminal defendant by showing another person admitted to the crime of which he is accused, FRE 804(b)(3) requires "corroborating circumstances [that] clearly indicate the trustworthiness of the statement." Criminal defense lawyers call this the "SODDI" defense: Some Other Dude Did It. It might feature a jailhouse snitch to testify he heard someone else admit that he committed the crime of which the defendant is accused. That "someone else" is called as a witness, and takes the Fifth Amendment, thus establishing his unavailability. In California, the jury would not have to be informed of the invocation of the self-incrimination privilege by the unavailable witness. See CEC 913. While CEC 1230 does not impose a requirement of corroboration as in FRE 804(b)(3), California courts are distrustful of exculpatory confessions by unavailable witnesses. They impose a requirement that a declaration against interest be "trustworthy." *People v. Coble*, 65 Cal.App.3d 187, 192–93 (1976). If the statement subjects a third person to greater criminal liability than the declarant, for example, it will be rejected even though it does subject the declarant to penal liability. *People v. Shipe*, 49 Cal.App.3d 343, 354 (1975).

CHAPTER TWENTY-SIX

Former Testimony

Focus on CEC 1290, 1291, 1292

1. The exception for former testimony in FRE 804(b)(1) includes testimony at another hearing of the same or a different case, as well as depositions taken in the same or a different case. The California definition of "former testimony", however, does *not* include a deposition taken in the same case. CEC 1290. That does not mean that a deposition taken in the same case will not be admissible, however. Its admissibility in civil cases is governed by Section 2025(u) of the California Code of Civil Procedure. Section 2025(u)(3) provides that if the deponent is unavailable as a witness, using the same standards as CEC 240, or if he resides more than 150 miles from the place of the trial, any party may use the deposition for any purpose. Section 2025(m)(2) provides that objections to the form of any question or answer are waived if they are not made at the deposition. When depositions are permitted in criminal cases, their admissibility is governed by California Penal Code Sections 1335–1345. California Penal Code Section 1345 permits a deposition to be read in evidence or shown to the jury if available on video, if the witness is unavailable within the meaning of CEC 240. The same objections can be made as if the witness were testifying in court, including objections to the form of the questions.

2. Under both FRE 804(b)(1) and CEC 1291, the former testimony exception can be used in *criminal* cases if the same party *against* whom the testimony is offered had an opportunity to cross-examine the witness in the former proceedings, with a similar motive. [**Example: G-31**]. Where the testimony was actually offered in evidence in the former proceeding by the party against whom it is now offered, the Federal Rules of Evidence and the California Evidence Code part company. FRE 804(b)(1) still requires a "similar motive" to develop the testimony in both proceedings. Relying upon this requirement, the Court in *United States v. Salerno,* 505 U.S. 317 (1992) held that a defen-

dant could not offer the exculpatory grand jury testimony of witnesses who invoked the Fifth Amendment at trial, unless he could show that the government had the same motive in both proceedings. CEC 1291, however, does not impose a "similar motive" requirement in these circumstances. Thus, a California court would reach the opposite result if presented with the *Salerno* facts. In the case of *People v. O.J. Simpson*, for example, the grand jury testimony of Thano Peratis, the nurse who drew blood from O.J. Simpson for DNA testing, was admitted against the prosecution when he became unavailable to testify due to illness. CEC 1291 also allows former testimony to be offered against a party who is a "successor in interest" to the party who offered it in the former proceeding.

3. In *civil* cases, both the Federal Rules of Evidence and the California Evidence Code provide a broader exception for former testimony, since the constitutional right to confront and cross-examine witnesses does not apply to civil cases. FRE 804(b)(1) allows former testimony if the same party, or a *predecessor in interest*, had an opportunity and similar motive to develop the testimony in the former proceeding. CEC 1292 does not require any legal relationship between the party against whom the testimony is offered and the party in the former proceeding, only that they had a similar interest and motive to cross-examine. The requirement that a different party have been a "predecessor in interest" was inserted into FRE 804(b)(1) by Congress, and the legislative history suggests a narrowly construed privity was intended.

4. FRE 804(b)(1) offers no guidance on which evidentiary objections are waived by failure to make them at the former proceeding. Federal Rules of Civil Procedure Rule 32(3)(A)-(B) contains waiver provisions governing the use of depositions, but does not apply where the former testimony was in a different proceeding. Under the California Evidence Code, different waiver standards apply to CEC 1291 and CEC 1292. Under CEC 1291, where the parties are generally the same in both proceedings, objections to the form the question which were not made in the former proceeding are waived, as are objections to competency or privilege which existed at the time the former testimony was given. Under CEC 1292, the only objections deemed waived are those based on competency or privilege which existed at the time the former testimony was given. In either case, objections based on relevance and extrinsic policy can be asserted, whether they were previously made or not. Where the former testimony contains hearsay, a hearsay objection can also be asserted. This is an example of "double hearsay." If, for example, the preliminary hearing testimony of a now unavailable witness is admitted

under the former testimony exception, and that witness recounted what a third person had said to him, that portion of the testimony could be excluded by a hearsay objection, unless another hearsay exception were found. See CEC 1201.

CHAPTER TWENTY-SEVEN

THE CONSTITUTIONAL RIGHT OF CONFRONTATION AND NEW HEARSAY EXCEPTIONS

Focus on CEC 1350, 1360, 1370 and 1380

1. Both the Federal Rules of Evidence and the California Evidence Code invite the judicial minting of new hearsay exceptions. The Federal Rules of Evidence include a "residual exception" in FRE 807, that allows a judge to admit a hearsay statement without an exception under FRE 803 or 804, but that is more probative than any other evidence of a material fact and has "equivalent circumstantial guarantees of trustworthiness." The California Evidence Code does not have a "residual" hearsay exception, but CEC 1200(b) says, "[e]xcept as provided by law, hearsay evidence is inadmissible." CEC 160 defines "law" to include "constitutional, statutory, and decisional law." Relying upon these provisions, the California Supreme Court upheld the carving out of a new non-statutory hearsay exception for statements by child abuse victims offered in child dependency cases. *In Re Cindy L.,* 17 Cal.4th 15 (1997). The legislature had created a child abuse exception in CEC 1360, but limited its applicability to criminal cases. The Court applied the same reliability requirements as CEC 1360, and found them adequate to protect the due process right of the defendants to reliable evidence. The constitutional right of confrontation, however, had no application since child dependency hearings are not criminal prosecutions.

2. The California legislature has added four new hearsay exceptions to the California Evidence Code since its original enactment. CEC 1350, 1360, 1370 and 1380. Curiously, three of them (all but 1370) are limited in their application to criminal cases, where the confrontation clause imposes the highest stan-

dards of reliability. If they meet this standard, why shouldn't they be available in civil cases as well? Applying the reasoning of *In Re Cindy L.,* why can't the courts simply extend the reach of CEC 1350 and 1370 to civil cases as well? All of the exceptions also require advance notice to the opposing party that the statement will be offered in evidence. There is, of course, no problem with Proposition 8 in enacting these exceptions. They do not *exclude* relevant evidence, but create exceptions to the rule of exclusion so the evidence can be admitted.

3. All four of the new statutory exceptions impose requirements of trustworthiness, but do so in different terms. Consider whether these terms are adequate to meet the constitutionally required showing of "particularized guarantees of trustworthiness."

4. CEC 1350 was already considered in our treatment of "unavailability" exceptions, Chapter 25, *supra.* It is the California equivalent of "forfeiture by wrongdoing" in FRE 804(b)(6). It requires that the statement of the unavailable declarant have been memorialized in a tape recording made by a law enforcement official, or in a written statement prepared by a law enforcement official and notarized in his presence. It also requires corroboration of the defendant's commission of the crime to which the statement relates, and imposes a general requirement that "the statement was made under circumstances which indicate its trustworthiness."

5. CEC 1360 creates a hearsay exception for children under the age of 12 describing an act of child abuse or neglect of which they were the victim. A finding is required that "the time, content, and circumstances of the statement provide sufficient indicia of reliability." If the child is unavailable to testify, there must be evidence of the child abuse or neglect that corroborates the statement.

6. CEC 1370, enacted in the wake of the O.J. Simpson trial, is *not* limited to domestic violence cases, however. It allows any statement narrating, describing or explaining the infliction or threat of any physical injury on the declarant. The statement must be in writing or recorded, or must have been made to a physician, nurse, paramedic or to a law enforcement official, and it must have been made at or near the time of the infliction or threat of the injury, and within the five years preceding the current action or proceeding.

The declarant must be unavailable, and the statement must have been made "under circumstances that would indicate its trustworthiness." Section 1370(b) provides that circumstances relevant to trustworthiness include whether the statement was made in contemplation of litigation, whether the declarant had a bias or motive for fabricating the statement, and whether the statement is corroborated by other evidence.

Prior to the O.J. Simpson trial, Judge Ito ruled that a "diary" written by Nicole Brown Simpson recounting some episodes of spousal abuse was inadmissible hearsay. It was written while divorce proceedings were pending, after a stipulation that any future physical abuse would abrogate an agreement as to the division of community property. Would CEC 1370 make it admissible? Could CEC 1370 be applied to an automobile accident victim who wrote out an account of how he was injured? Would a 911 operator qualify as a "law enforcement official" under CEC 1370?

The California Courts of Appeal have split on the question whether admission of a hearsay statement pursuant to the CEC 1370 exception would violate the confrontation clause. Admission was upheld in *People v. Hernandez*, 71 Cal.App.4th 417 (1999), and rejected in *People v. Kons*, 108 Cal.App.4th 514 (2003). [**Examples: G-12, K-12**].

7. CEC 1380 applies only to criminal prosecutions pursuant to California Penal Code Section 368, the California prohibition of "elder abuse." It creates a hearsay exception for the videotaped statement of an elderly victim who becomes unavailable. Admission of the statement requires a showing of particularized guarantees of trustworthiness and must be supported by corroborative evidence. Admission of evidence pursuant to the CEC 1380 hearsay exception was upheld against a confrontation claim in *People v. Tatum*, 108 Cal.App.4th 288 (2003).

8. To the extent they allow "testimonial" statements to be admitted that were never subjected to cross-examination, all four of the new California hearsay exceptions may violate the Confrontation Clause of the United States Constitution under the ruling of the U.S. Supreme Court in *Crawford v. Washington*, 541 U.S. 36 (2004). If the statements are elicited for use in court, as they ordinarily would be when they are elicited by a police officer, they would violate the absolute requirement of *Crawford* that testimonial statements made out of court be rejected unless the defendant has had an opportunity to cross-examine the declarant, regardless of circumstances suggesting "reliability." Thus far, California courts have found violations of a defendant's confrontation rights under *Crawford* where hearsay was admitted pursuant to CEC 1360 (*People v. Sisavath*, 118 Cal.App.4th 1396 (2004)) and CEC 1380 (*People v. Pirwani*, 119 Cal.App.4th 770 (2004)). The California Supreme Court has granted a hearing to consider whether a claimed confrontation violation by admitting hearsay pursuant to CEC 1370 was subject to "forfeiture by wrongdoing" in *People v. Giles*, No. S129852 (2005).

Chapter Twenty-Eight

Review of Hearsay Exceptions

The following chart organizes the California Hearsay Exceptions which correspond to each of the exceptions in Federal Rules 801, 803 and 804, summarizing the principle differences in the California exceptions.

HEARSAY EXCEPTION	FEDERAL RULE	CALIFORNIA EVID. CODE SECTION	CALIFORNIA DIFFERENCE
INCONSISTENT STATEMENTS	801(d)(1)(A)	1235, 770	Prior Statements need not be under oath.
CONSISTENT STATEMENTS	801(d)(1)(B)	1236, 791	May be abrogated by Prop. 8 in criminal cases.
IDENTIFICATION	801(d)(1)(C)	1238	Witness must vouch for prior identification.
PARTY ADMISSION	801(d)(2)(A)	1220	
ADOPTIVE ADMISSION	801(d)(2)(B)	1221	
AUTHORIZED ADMISSION	801(d)(2)(C)	1222	Authority must be independently proven.
AGENT ADMISSIONS	801(d)(2)(D)	1224	Admissibility is based upon theory of vicarious liability.
COCONSPIRATOR STATEMENTS	801(d)(2)(E)	1223	Membership in conspiracy must be independently proven; membership is question of conditional relevance.
PRESENT SENSE IMPRESSION	803(1)	1241	Declarant must be engaged in conduct.
EXCITED UTTERANCE	803(2)	1240	Startling event must be perceived by declarant.
EXISTING MENTAL CONDITION	803(3)	1250	Separate exception for wills in Section 1260.

28 · REVIEW OF HEARSAY EXCEPTIONS

HEARSAY EXCEPTION	FEDERAL RULE	CALIFORNIA EVID. CODE SECTION	CALIFORNIA DIFFERENCE
MEDICAL DIAGNOSIS	803(4)	[1251] [1253]	Need not be for medical diagnosis, but declarant must be unavailable and prior condition must be directly in issue. Limited to child abuse cases.
PAST RECOLLECTION RECORDED	803(5)	1237	Memorandum need not have been made or adopted by witness.
BUSINESS RECORDS	803(6)	1271	Opinions not explicitly included. Police reports not excluded as per U.S. v. Oates, 560 F.2d 45 (2nd Cir. 1977).
ABSENCE OF ENTRY IN BUSINESS RECORD	803(7)	1272	
OFFICIAL RECORDS	803(8)	1280	No exclusion of police reports. See People v. Parker, 8 Cal.App.4th 110 (1992).
ABSENCE OF ENTRY IN OFFICIAL RECORD	803(10)	1284	
UNAVAILABILITY EXCEPTIONS: DEFINING UNAVAILABILITY			
INVOKING PRIVILEGE	804(a)(1)	240(a)(1)	
CONTEMPTUOUS REFUSAL	804(a)(2)	—	Treated as "mental infirmity" in People v. Rojas, 15 Cal.3d 540 (1975).
LACK OF MEMORY	804(a)(3)	—	May be included in "mental infirmity."
DEATH OR INFIRMITY	804(a)(4)	240(a)(3)	
UNABLE TO PROCURE ATTENDANCE	804(a)(5)	240(a)(4), (5)	

HEARSAY EXCEPTION	FEDERAL RULE	CALIFORNIA EVID. CODE SECTION	CALIFORNIA DIFFERENCE
PRIOR TESTIMONY	804(b)(1)	1290–92	For depo. in same case, use CCP. If testimony previously offered by party, need not have same interest and motive. Procedure re waiver of Objections specified.
DYING DECLARATION	804(b)(2)	1242	Use in criminal cases not limited to homicides. Personal knowledge explicitly required.
DECLARATION AGAINST INTEREST	804(b)(3)	1230	Includes "social disgrace"; Exculpatory statements in criminal cases do not require corroboration, but subject to case law limitations.
FAMILY HISTORY	804(b)(4)	1310, 1311	
FORFEITURE BY WRONGDOING	804(b)(6)	1350	Limited to serious felony cases; Statement must be tape recorded or notarized, and corroborated.

Review Problem

The following statement of facts is taken from the court's opinion in *People v. Earnest*, 53 Cal.App.3d 734 (1975). On appeal, the defendant argued that all of the evidence connecting him with the crime was inadmissible hearsay. Identify any exceptions that might have been available to make the hearsay admissible, and then compare whether similar exceptions would have been available if the case had been tried in federal court.

The defendant Johnny Earnest was charged with soliciting a 15-year-old boy, Ruben Munoz, to burn down his house so he could collect insurance proceeds. Munoz died in the fire.

On January 25, 1974, Sergeant Robert Jones of the Woodland Police Department questioned defendant's stepfather, Paul May, in the Commanche County Jail in Lawton, Oklahoma. May told Jones that approximately a week before the fire, while riding in a car occupied by defendant and Ruben, he overheard a conversation between them about the burning of defendant's house. Defendant told Ruben that he wanted to get some money to buy into a small business or to buy two homes, live in one and rent the other. He asked Ruben how much money he wanted to set the house on fire. Ruben stated that they were friends and that he would take nothing for it, but defendant insisted that since he would thereby make money, Ruben should also make money. The fire was to occur approximately two to three months later, after defendant checked to make sure the fire insurance policy premium was paid. It was finally decided that Ruben would receive $100 for the burning.

Before the grand jury and at defendant's trial, May admitted making these statements to Sergeant Jones, but stated that except for riding in the car with Ruben and the defendant, they were all lies he manufactured because he was angry with defendant. He was angry because he had just been convicted of second-degree murder in Oklahoma and defendant's brother had 'turned state's evidence' against him in the case; he felt that defendant 'could have cleared him' if he had come to Oklahoma and testified. He added that Sergeant Jones offered to give him some information to help get a reversal of his conviction in return for his cooperation.

Linda Martinez, a former neighbor and friend of Ruben, testified to five conversations she had with Ruben prior to his death. Approximately three weeks prior to the fire, Ruben told her of his intention to set fire to defendant's residence. About a week later, Ruben and Linda engaged in a second conversation in which Ruben reiterated his intention to burn the residence, and also told her he would set the fire at 9:30 p.m. on a Saturday within the next two weeks, no one would be at home when he arrived; he would find a gasoline can on the back porch; the back door would be kicked in to suggest that the house had been broken into; all of the windows would be shut; and the gas would be left on inside the house. He told Linda he was to pour gasoline along the outside of the house and ignite it with a fuse constructed of a lit cigarette and a book of matches devised so as to provide him time to get away. Linda was also told that Ruben was to receive $100 for his efforts.

A third conversation occurred between Ruben and Linda approximately one week prior to the fire, during which Ruben stated that he would have some money by the following Monday for burning the house.

On the day of the fire, Ruben and Linda conversed on two occasions. In the first conversation she asked him if he still planned to set the fire. Receiving an affirmative response, she told him that if he did not change his mind she would have to tell either the police or his mother. He indicated he would think about it. The second conversation was by telephone at approximately 8:30 p.m. Ruben related that having thought the matter over, he had changed his mind and wouldn't go through with it.

Steven Fernandez testified that he was Ruben's cousin and that Ruben had lived with him and his wife Lisa prior to the fire. Sometime during the evening of the fire, Ruben asked Steven in the presence of Lisa, if Steven could give him a ride later in the evening. Later, Steven asked Ruben if he wanted to go, and Ruben responded that he wanted to wait until it was a little darker. Still later, Ruben said he was ready to leave, and Ruben and Steven departed. Ruben was not carrying anything.

After parking on Locust Street, within walking distance of defendant's Elm Street residence, Ruben declared, "I am going to burn this guy's house down." When Steven asked him why, Ruben responded, "Johnny's going to pay me for it." He also stated that Johnny wanted to collect on the fire insurance and that Ruben was to get $90 or $100 for his participation. Steven asked Ruben if he knew what he was doing, to which Ruben replied, "Johnny's got it all worked out." Ruben then outlined some of the details of the plan. He indicated that the back door was to be open with the appearance of having been forced, and a gasoline can and papers were to be available. He was to set the fire with a lit cigarette and a match book fuse. As Ruben left Steven he said, "Be right back." Five to seven minutes later, from his parked car, Steven saw the glow of the flames from the burning building. Mrs. Adelia Clark, next door neighbor to defendant, heard an explosion and observed flames erupt from the residence. She immediately telephoned the fire department. The firefighters, in addition to finding the boy's charred body, discovered a partially filled gasoline can in the house. There was also evidence that the back door had been forcibly opened. The physical evidence at the scene suggested that the boy had spread an inflammable liquid in two areas of the house; the liquid was ignited by one of two probable flame sources, the floor furnace or a pilot light on the water heater.

Defendant testified on his own behalf, and denied any involvement.

Part VI

Examining Witnesses

CHAPTER TWENTY-NINE

OPINIONS AND EXPERTS

Focus on CEC 720–21, 800–805

1. CEC 800, which states the general rule regarding opinions of lay witnesses, was identical to FRE 701 prior to its amendment in 2000. That amendment added FRE 701(c) to prevent evasion of FRE 702 by presenting "an expert witness in the guise of a layperson." Thus, one might fairly ask whether CEC 800, without the amendment, opens the door to such "evasion." The Law Revision Commission Comment to CEC 800 suggests that it might: "Section 800 does not make inadmissible an opinion that is admissible under existing law, even though the requirements of subdivisions (a) and (b) are not satisfied." In any event, opinions which are rationally based on a lay witness' observations are permitted. [**Examples: H-19, J-29, J-48, J-56**]. If they are merely based on speculation, however, they should be excluded. [**Examples: K-10, K-27, K-96**].

2. CEC 801, like FRE 702, requires that the testimony of an expert will "assist the trier of fact." California cases have permitted experts to testify on the fallibility of eye witness identifications, *People v. McDonald* (1984) 37 Cal.3d 351, the "rape trauma syndrome," *People v. Bledsoe* (1984) 36 Cal.3d 236, and the "child sexual abuse accommodation syndrome," *People v, Bowker* (1988) 203 Cal.App.3d 385. There is a specific section of the California Evidence Code addressing the admissibility of expert testimony regarding the "battered women's syndrome." CEC 1107. "Syndrome" testimony can be used to explain the behavior of the victim, but cannot be used to identify the perpetrator, or to offer an opinion that the victim has, in fact, been raped or abused. [**Examples: C-60, L-50**].

3. The requirements to qualify an expert witness appear in CEC 720. The qualification of an expert witness is a preliminary question decided by the judge, pursuant to CEC 405. Because qualifications will also affect the weight to be given to the expert's opinion by the jury, a judge will ordinarily permit the foundation to qualify the expert to be presented while the jury is present. Under CEC 720, a party has a right to insist that the qualifications of the ex-

pert be shown before the witness testifies. There is no similar limit upon the judge's discretion as to order of proof under the Federal Rules. FRE 611(a). [**Examples: A-7, D-35, E-13, E-32, E-36, J-48, J-60, K-70**]. A challenge to the expert's qualifications is not an attack on his character, which might be prohibited by the rules on character evidence. The challenge to qualifications might include specific acts of misconduct, such as prior negligence, but they are offered for the limited purpose of assessing the credibility and weight to be given to his expert opinions. [**Example: K-85**]. A special rule defines who is permitted to give opinions regarding the value of property. CEC 813. [**Example: G-14**].

4. California does not follow the *Daubert* standard for scientific and technical evidence now embodied in FRE 702. Instead, California still follows the "general acceptance" test established in *Frye v. United States,* 293 Fed. 1013 (D.C. Cir. 1923). It is known in California as the "Kelly-Frye" test, based upon its explication in *People v. Kelly* 17 Cal.3d 24 (1976). The *Daubert* standard was explicitly rejected by the California Supreme Court in *People v. Leahy* 8 Cal.4th 587 (1994). [**Examples: C-43, H-11, H-58**].

5. Just as under FRE 703, the California Evidence Code permits an expert to base his opinion upon hearsay information "of a type that reasonably may be relied upon by an expert in forming an opinion upon the subject to which his testimony relates." CEC 801(b). Under CEC 804, however, the adverse party may call and cross-examine another person whose statement or opinion is relied upon by the expert. CEC 352 may impose a significant limitation upon the admissibility of hearsay relied upon by the expert, where there is substantial danger that the hearsay will be misused by the jury as evidence to prove the truth of what was asserted. For example, in *People v. Coleman* 38 Cal.3d 69 (1985), the mental health experts who were called to testify about the defendant's mental condition had considered letters written by his deceased wife (the murder victim) accusing him of hurting her and threatening to kill her and the children. The court held that it was an abuse of discretion under CEC 352 to permit cross examination as to the contents of the letters. [**Examples: C-49, C-51, F-33, F-40, H-62**].

6. Both FRE 704 and CEC 805 permit opinions on the "ultimate conclusion." But the opinion, whether offered by a lay person or an expert, may still be objectionable as "conclusory" if it is not rationally based upon the observations of the lay witness, or the expertise of the expert witness. A physician testifying whether observed trauma was consistent with rape, for example, could not testify as to the identity of the rapist. [**Examples: D-26, E-38, F-36, G-76, H-80, L-2**]. Under the Federal Rules, the general rule *permitting* opinions on ultimate issues contains an important exception to exclude the opin-

ions of psychiatrists in criminal cases opining whether the defendant had the requisite mental state. FRE 704. This limitation was the product of Congressional outrage over the acquittal of John Hinckley for the attempted assassination of President Ronald Reagan. While CEC 805 does not contain a similar exception, it will be found in Section 29 of the California Penal Code. The California exception was also motivated by outrage over the verdict in a high-profile political assassination case: the manslaughter verdict returned against Dan White for the assassination of San Francisco Mayor George Moscone.

7. The California Evidence Code originally imposed more stringent limitations than the Federal Rules of Evidence upon cross-examination of experts based on texts and treatises. FRE 803(18) creates a broad hearsay exception for statements contained in published treatises which are "called to the attention" of an expert in cross-examination (or relied upon by him in direct examination), as long as they are established as reliable authority by the witness *or by other expert testimony or by judicial notice.* As originally enacted, CEC 721(b) prohibited cross-examination of experts from a text or treatise not admitted in evidence, unless the expert considered it or relied upon it in forming his opinion. There is a very limited hearsay exception for books offered to prove "facts of general notoriety and interest" in CEC 1341. In 1997, however, CEC 721(b) was amended to include publications established as reliable authority by "the witness or by other expert testimony or by judicial notice," paralleling the federal rule. However, the amendment to 721(b) does not create a hearsay exception. Also, under CEC 452(h), a court has discretion to take judicial notice only of facts and propositions "that are not reasonable subject to dispute and are capable of immediate and accurate determination by resort to source of reasonably indisputable accuracy." Thus, the California rule may permit inquiry on cross-examination, but the cited portion of the text or treatise will not be admitted as evidence to prove the truth of what is asserted unless it qualifies under an exception to the hearsay rule. [**Example: L-64**].

Where the inquiry is to test the credibility of the expert by showing that he is unfamiliar with the opinions of other experts in his field, the limitations of CEC 721(b) may be ignored. At least they were by the California Supreme Court in deciding *People v. Bell* (1989) 49 Cal.3d 502, 532. The Court declared: "[A] party seeking to attack the credibility of [an] expert may bring to the attention of the jury material relevant to the issue on which the expert has offered an opinion [and] of which the expert was *unaware* or which he did *not* consider." [**Examples: F-45, K-83**].

8. Experts are subject to the same impeachment as any other witness, including a showing of bias. CEC 722(b) permits inquiry into the compensation paid to an expert. [**Examples: J-81, K-77**].

9. Prior to the adoption of the Federal Rules of Evidence and the California Evidence Code, many courts required every factual assumption upon which an expert opinion was based to be stated in a hypothetical question. For example:

> "Doctor, assuming a twenty-eight year old female in previous good health is found floating in a swimming pool, and assume an autopsy reveals water in her lungs and no other unusual marks or signs of trauma on her body, do you have an opinion as to the cause of death?"

Under both CEC 802 and FRE 705, such a ritual is no longer necessary. The lawyer can elicit the expert's opinion at the outset of his testimony, then elicit the reasons for the opinion.

Chapter Thirty

Authentication

Focus on CEC 250, 1400–1402

1. FRE 901 requires authentication or identification of *any* tangible evidence, while CEC 1400 refers only to the authentication of a "writing." "Writing" is defined in CEC 250 in virtually the same terms as FRE 1001(1). As the Law Revision Commission Comment to CEC 1400 points out, however, a preliminary showing of relevance is required for the admission of any tangible object. To avoid confusion, refer to this preliminary showing as "authentication" only when dealing with writings; refer to it as "identification" when dealing with other tangible objects. Evidence of the contents of a telephone call or an email message ordinarily requires the witness to identify the caller or sender, and describe how she knew his identity. [**Examples: A-9, C-32, H-34, J-9**].

2. Under both the Federal Rules of Evidence and the California Evidence Code, authentication or identification are matters of conditional relevance, requiring evidence sufficient to sustain a finding by the jury, pursuant to FRE 104(b) or CEC 403.

3. The California Evidence Code does not provide for "self-authentication" as permitted under FRE 902. Sections 1410–1421 suggest a number of alternatives to authenticate a writing, including the testimony of a witness who saw the writing made [CEC 1413], handwriting analysis evidence [CEC 1415–19], evidence the writing was a reply to a previous communication [CEC 1420], or evidence of contents unlikely to be known by anyone other than the purported author [CEC 1421]. An admission of authenticity by the party against whom it is offered will also suffice [CEC 1414], and can frequently be obtained in pretrial discovery. See, *e.g.*, Fed. R. of Civ. Procedure, Rule 36, 37 (c).

4. Authentication is *not* a hearsay exception, of course. In addition to authenticating a writing, if it is offered to prove the truth of its contents, a hearsay exception must be found. If it was authored by the party against whom it is offered, it will qualify as an admission. If it was prepared in the

ordinary course of business or official activity, it may qualify as a business or official record.

Chapter Thirty-One

The Best Evidence and Secondary Evidence Rules

Focus on CEC 1520–23

1. There is no rule that requires a party to present the "best" or strongest evidence available to prove a contested fact. A jury can be instructed in accordance with CEC 412 that evidence should be viewed with distrust if a party offers weak evidence when stronger evidence was available, but that should not be confused with the "best evidence" rule. The "best evidence" rule only applies to writings offered as evidence, and requires the party to account for the original writing if secondary evidence is offered to prove its contents. The California Evidence Code has replaced the "best evidence" rule with a "secondary evidence" rule that shifts the burden to the opposing party to exclude secondary evidence of a writing.
2. The most common violation of the "best evidence" rule occurs when a witness offers an oral description of the contents of a writing. California's "secondary evidence" rule also excludes oral testimony of the contents of a writing, with several exceptions spelled out in CEC 1523. [**Examples: B-10, C-53, D-12, E-18, F-52, G-12, G-14, G-86, H-11, H-21, H-34, K-97, L-34**].
3. The "secondary evidence" rule was adopted by a two-thirds vote of the California legislature in 1998, so even though it excludes relevant evidence, it is fully applicable in criminal cases despite Proposition 8.
4. Unlike the requirement of authentication, compliance with the secondary evidence rule is not an issue of conditional relevance. It is decided by the judge pursuant to CEC 405.
5. The most significant difference between the Federal Rules of Evidence "best evidence" rule and the California Evidence Code "secondary evidence" rule occurs when the original is not available. Under FRE 1004, the *proponent* must show that all originals are lost or destroyed before offering secondary evidence

other than a duplicate. A duplicate is admissible, unless the *opponent* raises a genuine question as to authenticity of the original, or it would be "unfair" to admit the duplicate in lieu of the original. FRE 1003.

Under the California Evidence Code, no distinction is made between "duplicates" or other secondary evidence. *Any* secondary evidence will be admitted, unless the opponent raises a genuine dispute as to the terms of the writing and justice requires its exclusion, or admission of the evidence would be unfair. CEC 1521. [**Examples: D-46, J-56**].

6. An additional limitation is imposed upon the use of secondary evidence in *criminal* cases by CEC 1522. Since narrower discovery rules apply to criminal cases, CEC 1522 precludes use of secondary evidence if the original is in the possession of the proponent, and the proponent has not made it reasonably available for inspection. This rule does not apply to a duplicate.

7. A "duplicate" is defined in CEC 260 in the same terms as FRE 1001(4): a counterpart produced by the same impression as the original, or from the same matrix, or by means of photography or mechanical or electronic re-recording or chemical reproduction.

Chapter Thirty-Two

Evidentiary Objections

Focus on CEC 353–356, 764–767

1. Merely stating an objection without specifying the grounds is insufficient to preserve the issue for appeal. Even if hearsay or irrelevant evidence is erroneously admitted, the ruling will be sustained on appeal if the objection did not specify that the evidence was "hearsay" or "irrelevant." CEC 353. On the other hand, if a general objection is *sustained,* the ruling excluding the evidence will be upheld if there is any ground available to sustain it. CEC 354. Thus, counsel should request the court to specify the grounds for the ruling, and make an offer of proof.
2. An objection should be asserted to a *question* that it "calls for" hearsay or "calls for" irrelevant evidence. If the question has been answered, the objection should be accompanied by a motion to strike, and a request that the jury be instructed to disregard the answer. An objection to an answer and a motion to strike may be made by the examining attorney, but can be met with an argument that the attorney "opened the door" by his question, and the answer was responsive to the question. [**Example: K-18**].
3. If evidence is admitted for a limited purpose, the court is required to give a limiting instruction to the jury. CEC 355. The instruction is most effective if it is given when the evidence is admitted. Failure to request a limiting instruction ordinarily waives any error in failure to give it.
4. A Motion in Limine can be brought by either side to obtain an advance ruling on the admissibility of evidence. While such motions are encouraged, it is a misuse of the motion to attempt to compel a witness or a party to conform trial testimony to a preconceived factual scenario based on testimony given during pretrial discovery. *Kelly v. New West Federal Savings,* 49 Cal.App.4th 659 (1996). Just as under FRE 103(a)(2) as amended in 2000, there is no need to renew an objection in California if an in limine ruling addressed the admission of a particular item of evidence. *People v. Rowland,* 4 Cal.4th 238, 264 n.3 (1992); *People v. Jennings,* 46 Cal.3d 963, 775 n.3 (1988).

the court in an in limine ruling indicates it will permit a witness to be impeached with a prior conviction, counsel presenting the witness frequently elects, as a tactical matter, to "take the sting out" by eliciting the prior conviction himself. In *Ohler v. United States*, 529 U.S. 753 (2000), the U.S. Supreme Court put the sting back in for federal cases, by holding that an objection is waived when counsel elicits the objectionable material himself. California courts have not yet addressed the question of whether an *Ohler* type waiver will be imposed in California. [**Example: H-77**].

5. Although the rules excluding character evidence are based upon principles of relevancy, a mere objection based on relevancy will not preserve the error. The objection should specify that the evidence violates a specific rule excluding character evidence. *People v. Escobar*, 48 Cal.App.4th 999 (1996). Relevancy objections should routinely include a request to exclude the evidence under Section 352. The Section 352 objection will be waived if it is not explicitly asserted. A mere objection that the evidence is "irrelevant" will not preserve for appellate review the argument that the judge abused his or her discretion by admitting the evidence because its probative value was outweighed by considerations of prejudice or confusion of the jury.

6. An objection of "lack of foundation" is ordinarily not sufficient to preserve an issue for appeal. If the missing foundation is required to qualify for a hearsay exception, the proper objection is that the evidence is hearsay.

7. An objection that a question is "leading" is only appropriate during direct or redirect examination. Leading questions are permitted on cross and recross examination. CEC 767(a). A leading question is one that suggests the answer counsel seeks, usually in the form of a "yes" or "no" answer. CEC 764. A judge's discretion to permit leading questions on direct is sharply limited to "special circumstances where the interests of justice require," with the exception of children under 10 in child abuse cases. CEC 767(b).

8. The opposite of a leading question is one that calls for a narrative, which is equally objectionable since it gives counsel no warning of inadmissible matter coming in. Objection that a question calls for a narrative answer can be made pursuant to CEC 765.

9. At common law, only the examining party could object that an answer was non-responsive. CEC 766 permits either party to object and move to strike the answer.

10. Where testimony becomes repetitious, an objection that a question was "asked and answered" may be appropriate. CEC 774 prohibits reexamining a witness as to the same matter without leave of court.

11. When a question incorporates an argumentative comparison, an objection that the question is "argumentative" is appropriate. For example, "How can you remember that you left before 2 a.m., when you can't remember what time you arrived?" [**Examples: A-47, G-80**].

12. Cross examination is limited to the scope of direct examination. CEC 761. If counsel ventures into new areas on cross examination, an objection that the questions are beyond the scope of direct examination should be asserted. While counsel can request the Court for permission to take the witness on direct examination, CEC 772(c), leading questions will not be permitted. Thus, the objection preserves the critical limitation of leading questions to cross examination. [**Example: H-25**].

13. When counsel for one side "opens the door" by eliciting inadmissible evidence, it can be rebutted with evidence of the same character. Frequently, a lawyer will prefer to offer rebuttal evidence, rather than objecting to exclude the inadmissible evidence. [**Example: J-5**].

14. An objection that the admission of evidence violates rights under the State or Federal constitutions must be explicitly asserted. This is particularly important with hearsay objections where a violation of the constitutional right of confrontation is asserted. *People v. Bolin*, 18 Cal.4th 297, 319 (1998); *People v. Carpenter*, 15 Cal.4th 312, 385 (1997).

15. There is no rule against "collateral impeachment" under the California Evidence Code. Evidence to contradict a witness' testimony and show that a fact he or she testified to is not true is always relevant, but the judge has discretion to exclude it under CEC 352 if its probative value is substantially outweighed by the dangers of prejudice, confusion or undue consumption of time. Thus, objections that used to be made that impeachment was "collateral" to the issues in the lawsuit are now simply made as CEC 352 objections. [**Example: L-92**].

16. In order to preserve a federal constitutional claim for review in federal court, a criminal defense lawyer in state court must "exhaust" state remedies by explicitly asserting the federal claim in state court. A California case offers an excellent example. In *Duncan v. Henry*, 513 U.S. 364, the defendant was on trial for allegedly molesting a 5-year-old child. The prosecution offered the testimony of the parent of another child, who claimed Henry had also molested her child twenty years previously. The defense lawyer unsuccessfully argued that the prejudicial impact of this evidence outweighed its probative value, and it should be excluded pursuant to CEC 352, the equivalent of FRE 403. The testimony was admitted and Henry was convicted. On direct appeal, the California appellate court found admission of the evidence was error, but concluded it was harmless. Henry then petitioned for a writ of habeas corpus

in federal court, arguing the evidence was not harmless and its admission denied him due process of law in violation of his federal constitutional rights. The petition was granted, a ruling which was upheld by the U.S. Court of Appeals for the Ninth Circuit. But the U.S. Supreme Court summarily reversed the case, holding that Henry never explicitly raised the federal due process issue in state court, and thus did not "exhaust" his claim. By not intoning the magic words "federal due process", the issue was lost and Henry's claim for habeas relief went with it. In dissenting, Justice John Paul Stevens bluntly assessed the impact of this ruling: the case "tightens the pleading screws...to hold that the exhaustion doctrine includes an exact labeling requirement." 513 U.S. at 368.

The point takes on added significance in the wake of *Crawford v. Washington,* 541 U.S. 36 (2004). The federal constitutional right of confrontation may be lost if it is not explicitly asserted in state court. That's exactly what happened to one of the two codefendants in *Idaho v. Wright,* 497 U.S. 805 (1990). Both were convicted of child molestation. The Idaho Supreme Court rejected the confrontation claim of codefendant Giles, because only a hearsay objection had been raised, while the conviction of codefendant Wright was reversed on confrontation grounds, a ruling subsequently affirmed by the U.S. Supreme Court. Not federalizing his claim cost Giles a reversal of his conviction.

A competent trial lawyer who reads these cases will accompany every hearsay objection at trial with an objection that admission of the evidence violates his or her client's federal [and state] constitutional right of confrontation. Every relevancy objection will include, in addition to an invocation of the equivalent of the FRE 403 appeal to the discretion of the judge to exclude evidence because its probative value is substantially outweighed by its prejudicial impact, a constitutional objection that the admission of the evidence will violate his or her client's right to due process of law. Trial judges might not have much patience with the additional time it will take to hear all these objections, but Chuck Sevilla of San Diego, California has come up with an ingenious solution. He calls it the "Mantra Motion."

The "Mantra Motion" should be filed at the outset of the trial, to secure the Court's agreement to a simplified and expedited form of making objections for the record. The Court should be informed that the purpose of the motion is to save the court's time, to minimize the need for sidebar conferences, and to avoid needless interruption of opposing counsel's presentation of his or her case. Sevilla suggests that the defense request permission to make constitutional objections in the following manner:

Option #1: The simplest alternative would make every hearsay, relevance or "403" objection deemed to have been also made under the due process clause of the 5th and 14th Amendment and under the confrontation clause of the 6th and 14th Amendments. (This requires agreement by the court on the record.)

Option #2: If option #1 is rejected, than a "by the numbers" alternative is proposed:

A due process objection would be made by simply adding "5" to the evidentiary objection. A confrontation objection would be made by adding "6" to the evidentiary objection. When objecting to unconstitutional argument to the jury by the prosecutor, counsel would simply specify "prosecution error." More specifically, the motion explains the grounds of the objections to incorporated in the numerical recitations:

A "5" objection encompasses the due process guarantee of a fair trial, as guaranteed by the Fifth Amendment of the U.S. Constitution, made applicable to the states through the 14th Amendment. A "6" objection includes both state and federal constitutional guarantees of the rights to confront and cross-examine witnesses. An "8" objection covers the eighth amendment protection against cruel and unusual punishment as well as the parallel protection under the state constitution. A "prosecution error" objection includes the assertion that the prosecutor's comment is irrelevant, inflammatory and prejudicial, and violates the defendant's state and federal constitutional rights to a fair trial under the Fifth and Fourteenth Amendments to the U.S. Constitution, as well as the Sixth Amendment right to confrontation and cross-examination. The error has "so infected the trial with unfairness as to make any resulting conviction a denial of due process." *Donnelly v. De Christoforo*, 416 U.S. 637, 643 (1974). The objection includes a request the court assign this as misconduct, strike the offending comments, and admonish the jury to disregard it. If the court will not do that, a mistrial is requested.

The "Mantra Motion" is a "win-win" motion for the trial judge, since it speeds up the trial process with no sacrifice in the accuracy and completeness of the record. Even if the incorporated or "by the number" objections are all denied, the record is preserved so these claims can be asserted in a habeas petition in federal court. If the "Mantra Motion" is denied, competent counsel is left with no choice but to recite all of the federal and state constitutional grounds available each time he or she objects. Remember to make all of your objections together at the same time, however. Trial judges (and juries) quickly tire of counsel who repeatedly make a long series of objections one at a time.

Part VII

Privileges

Chapter Thirty-Three

Privileges in General

Focus on CEC 900–920

1. Thirteen separate and distinct privileges are recognized in Chapter Four of the California Evidence Code, and two more elsewhere in the Evidence Code (Privileges for news reporters in CEC 1070 and for mediation participants in CEC 1119 and 1121). Still other privileges are found in other California Codes. See, *e.g.*, Calif. Code of Civil Procedure §2018(b) (Privilege for attorney work product). The courts are not free to recognize additional privileges. Section 911 of the California Evidence Code requires *statutory* recognition for a privilege.

2. There is a broad exception for all existing privileges in Proposition Eight, so privileges apply in criminal proceedings even though they exclude relevant evidence. Newly enacted privileges cannot be applied in criminal cases, however, unless they were enacted by a two-thirds vote of the legislature.

3. The initial question with respect to the applicability of any privilege will be, "who is entitled to assert it?" In California, the "holder" of each privilege is defined in the statutory recognition of the privilege. *See, e.g.*, CEC 953, 993. Frequently, the holder of the privilege is not a party to the lawsuit. If a privilege is asserted by a witness, and the court overrules the privilege and orders the witness to testify, the parties have no standing to claim the ruling was erroneous. CEC 918. If the privilege is sustained, however, the party presenting the testimony is deprived of relevant evidence and can challenge the ruling on appeal. Where the holder of a privilege is neither a party nor a witness, the presiding officer may nonetheless recognize a privilege and exclude information subject to the privilege. CEC 916.

4. Any voluntary substantial disclosure of privileged information by a holder will waive the privilege, but if there are *joint* holders (as in spousal communications), a waiver by one holder does not affect the right of another holder to claim the privilege. CEC 912. Nor is the privilege waived if disclosure is coerced. If a claim of privilege is erroneously denied, and disclosure is made pur-

suant to a court order, the disclosure is coerced and does not operate as a waiver of the privilege. CEC 918. [Example: L-84].

5. The availability of a privilege is a preliminary question decided by the judge pursuant to CEC 405. In ruling on a claim of privilege, the judge must presume that a communication was made in confidence, and the opponent of the claim of privilege has the burden of proof to show the communication was not confidential. CEC 917. With the exceptions noted below, the judge may not require disclosure of the communication in order to rule on the claim of privilege. CEC 915.

6. Some privileges are limited by the requirement that the judge "balance" the need for confidentiality against the need for disclosure. *See* Privilege for official information [CEC 1040], Privilege for identity of informant [CEC 1041], Privilege for trade secrets [CEC 1060], and Privilege for attorney work product [Code of Civ. Proc. §2018(b)]. In ruling on these privileges, the judge may require disclosure of the privileged information in an *in camera* proceeding from which the parties are excluded. CEC 915(b).

7. If an "eavesdropper" intercepts privileged communications without the consent of the parties, the privilege can still be asserted to prevent disclosure. *See* Law Revision Commission Comment, CEC 954. But the making of a communication under circumstances where others could easily overhear it is evidence that the communication was not intended to be confidential. *Sharon v. Sharon* 79 Cal. 633, 677 (1889).

8. The exercise of a privilege may not be the subject of comment by judge or counsel, and no adverse inference is permitted by the trier of fact with regard to the credibility of the witness or any other issue in the proceeding. CEC 913. [Example: G-31].

9. If a claim of privilege is overruled, a witness may be ordered by the court to be a witness, to disclose any matter that was claimed to be privileged, or to produce any writing, object or other thing that was claimed to be privileged. A refusal to obey the order is punishable as contempt of court. Note that a sustained claim of privilege would render the witness "unavailable as a witness" for the purpose of utilizing hearsay exceptions, CEC 240(a)(1), but a contemptuous refusal to testify would not, unless it was the product of "mental illness or infirmity." CEC 240(a)(3). See *People v. Rojas* (1975) 13 Cal.3d 540.

10. There are two different marital privileges, which should not be confused. There is a privilege which protects confidential communications between spouses during their marriage, and there is a privilege not be called as a witness against one's spouse during the marriage. The privilege for confidential communications survives the marriage, and one can prevent the disclosure of

marital communications even after the marriage has ended in divorce. But the privilege not to testify does not survive the marriage. The privilege not to testify extends even to crimes committed before the marriage, but CEC 972(f) creates an exception where knowledge of the crime was acquired before the marriage and the witness knew of the spouse's arrest or formal charge prior to the marriage. [**Examples:** C-32, F-79, G-31].

Chapter Thirty-Four

The Attorney-Client Privilege

Focus on CEC 950–962

1. The California attorney-client privilege protects confidential communications between client and lawyer. CEC 954. While the client is the holder of the privilege, CEC 953, the lawyer who received or made a communication subject to the privilege is *required* to assert the privilege on the client's behalf whenever he or she is present when disclosure is sought. CEC 955.

2. The privilege also protects the fact that a document was communicated to the client by his lawyer. In *In Re Navarro* (1979) 93 Cal.App.3d 325, the court upheld a claim of attorney-client privilege by a deputy public defender who was asked if she showed an arrest report to her client, a jail inmate charged with murdering a fellow inmate who was identified as a witness in the arrest report.

3. The "crime or fraud exception" to the attorney-client privilege only applies where the services of the attorney were sought to assist in the perpetration of the crime or fraud. CEC 956. The mere fact that the client discloses his intent to commit a crime or fraud in the future does not bring the communication within the exception. If the client reveals an intention to commit a crime, and the lawyer believes that it is likely to result in death or serious bodily harm to another, and that disclosure is necessary to prevent it, there is an exception to the privilege. CEC 956.5. This exception is also incorporated as an exception to the ethical obligation imposed upon an attorney by Section 6068(e) of the California Business and Professions Code, to maintain inviolate the confidence and preserve the secrets of his or her client. Thus, the lawyer who reveals a communication subject to CEC 956.5 would not be subject to professional discipline. Disclosure remains voluntary, however; it is not compulsory. Whether failure to disclose would subject an attorney to liability under *Tarasoff v. Re-*

gents of the University of California 17 Cal.3d 425 (1976), however, remains an open question.

4. In *Swidler & Berlin v. United States* 524 U.S. 399 (1998), the U.S. Supreme Court held that the common law attorney-client privilege applicable in federal cases survives the death of the client. The California attorney-client privilege, however, can only be claimed if there is a holder of the privilege in existence. CEC 954(c). The personal representative of a dead client is a holder of the privilege, CEC 953, but the privilege ceases to exist when the client's estate is finally distributed and his personal representative is discharged. *See* Law Revision Commission Comment, CEC 954.

5. Corporate counsel represent the corporation, and the attorney-client privilege is held by the corporation, not the individual employees or officers with whom the corporate counsel communicates. The breadth of protection which can be asserted *by the corporation* is significantly different between the common law privilege applied by the federal courts, and the California privilege. In *Upjohn Co. v. United States* 449 U.S. 383 (1981), the court rejected a "control group" test that would limit the privilege to the corporate officers who rely upon the advice of corporate counsel. It held that the privilege protected the results of interviews and questionnaires of all corporate employees conducted by corporate counsel in order to give legal advice. The California privilege is not construed this broadly. In *Chadbourne v. Superior Court* (1964) 60 Cal.2d 723, the Court held that when an employee has been a witness to matters requiring communication to corporate counsel, and has no connection with those matters other than as a witness, he is an independent witness, and the fact that the employer requires him to make a statement for transmittal to corporate counsel does not make the statement subject to the attorney-client privilege. [**Example: B-53**].

6. A corporate decision to waive the protection of its attorney-client privilege can result in full disclosure of communications among corporate officers, employees and corporate counsel. Thus, it is important that corporate counsel not mislead employees into believing he is serving as *their* lawyer.

7. An exception to the attorney-client privilege arises when the communication is relevant to an issue of breach, by either the lawyer or the client, of a duty arising from the lawyer-client relationship. CEC 958. Thus, if a client sues a lawyer for malpractice, or challenges a criminal conviction based upon a claim of incompetence of counsel, there is no privilege for communications relevant to the dispute. The same principle applies to a breach of duty by the client. Thus, a lawyer seeking to collect an unpaid fee can attach assets of which he became aware in confidential communications.

8. Ordinarily, concurrent representation of two clients upon a matter of common interest is precluded by the ethical prohibition against representation of conflicting interests, but that protection can be waived by the client. If it is, neither client can claim the attorney-client privilege against the other in litigation between them. CEC 962.

Part VIII

Presumptions and Judicial Notice

Chapter Thirty-Five

Presumptions

Focus on CEC 600–670

1. Direct evidence is evidence that directly proves a fact without an inference. CEC 410. Circumstantial evidence gives rise to an inference that a fact is true. A *presumption* is simply a *mandatory* inference, which requires an inference that a fact is true once the predicate fact giving rise to the inference is proven. But "mandatory" can mean two different things: it can mean the judge is required to make the inference, in ruling on a Motion for a Directed Verdict, or it can mean the jury is required to make the inference in its evaluation of the evidence.

2. To say a presumption is "rebuttable" means that evidence can be offered to show the inferred fact is *not* true. A conclusive presumption is not rebuttable. If the predicate fact giving rise to the inference is found to be true, then the presumed fact *must* also be found to be true, and any evidence to the contrary would be irrelevant and inadmissible. There are only three conclusive presumptions in the California Evidence Code, appearing in Sections 622–24.

3. With respect to rebuttable presumptions, the California Evidence Code recognizes and creates two types: a presumption affecting the burden of producing evidence, and a presumption affecting the burden of proof. The presumption affecting the burden of producing evidence is the "bursting bubble" type, frequently referred to as the "Thayer type" in honor of Professor Thayer, who thought that all presumptions should have this effect. This is also the effect attributed to all presumptions in civil cases under FRE 301, unless modified by statute. This presumption requires the fact finder to find that the presumed fact is true once the predicate fact is proven, unless the opposing party produces some evidence to rebut the presumed fact. If he does, then the presumption disappears, or "bursts." The finder of fact then simply weighs the inference against the countering evidence, with the burden of proof unaffected

and the presumption no longer having any effect. The presumptions which affect the burden of producing evidence appear in Sections 630–647 of the California Evidence Code.

The presumption affecting the burden of proof, often referred to as the "Morgan type" in honor of Professor Morgan, who thought that all presumptions should have this effect, actually shifts the burden of disproving the presumed fact to the opposing party. He must then offer sufficient evidence rebutting the presumption to meet the burden of proof. The presumptions which shift the burden of proof appear in Sections 662–670 of the California Evidence Code.

4. Many presumptions created by California law appear elsewhere than in the Evidence Code. The Evidence Code determines what evidentiary effect they have, however.

Conclusive presumptions must be declared by law to be conclusive. CEC 620. Presumptions affecting the burden of producing evidence are established to implement no public policy other than facilitating the resolution of the dispute in which they are applied. CEC 603. Presumptions affecting the burden of proof are established to implement some public policy which is extrinsic to the dispute, such as promoting marriage and family relationships or the security of property rights. CEC 605.

5. In criminal cases, presumptions cannot undercut the prosecution's burden of proving the case beyond a reasonable doubt. Thus, a burden-shifting presumption cannot be applied in a criminal case unless the predicate fact is found beyond a reasonable doubt. The defendant's burden is then only to raise a reasonable doubt as to the presumed fact.
CEC 607.

Presumption Review Problem

Assume that Child (C) has brought suit against his father's Wife (and his mother) (W), to recover a valuable diamond. C offers evidence tending to establish the following facts:

C1: Child's Father (A) purchased the diamond with his own, personal funds on October 1, 1995.

C2: On December 1, 1995, A delivered the diamond to W, his wife.

C3: A valid holographic will dated December 10, 1995, in A's handwriting, makes a specific bequest of the same diamond "to my surviving children."

C4: On January 1, 1996, A disappeared when his yacht sank in a storm in the Mediterranean Sea.

C5: C was born on October 8, 1970, to W, who was married to A and living with him. No other children were born during the marriage, which was A's only marriage.

W then offers the following evidence:

W1: A postcard signed by A, postmarked July 15, 1998, mailed from Casablanca.

W2: The testimony of K, who says she saw A in a Casablanca restaurant in July of 2002.

W3: W's own testimony, that A actually wrote the will November 10, 1995 and post-dated it.

W4: W's own testimony that A was impotent, and never consummated their marriage.

W5: The testimony of a physician that C's blood type is incompatible with A's blood type, rendering it impossible for A to be C's father.

All of W's evidence is reasonably disputable. How should the judge instruct the jury to resolve the factual disputes, in light of the following presumptions:

CEC 632: A thing delivered by one to another is presumed to have belonged to the latter.

CEC 637: The things which a person possesses are presumed to be owned by him.

CEC 638: A person who exercises acts of ownership over property is presumed to be the owner of it.

CEC 640: A writing is presumed to have been truly dated.

CEC 667: A person not heard from in five years is presumed to be dead.

Calif. Family Code Section 7540: "...the child of a wife cohabiting with her husband, who is not impotent or sterile, is conclusively presumed to be a child of the marriage."

Analysis

In order to win his lawsuit and recover the diamond under the will, C must prove that A is dead, that he is A's child, and that the diamond belonged to A at the time of his death.

Identify the presumptions that C's evidence would give rise to. Are they conclusive? Do they merely create a burden to produce evidence, or do they shift the burden of proof on any particular issues? Analyze the evidence produced by W to determine if it challenges the predicate fact or the presumed fact. If it challenges the presumed fact, does it make the presumption "disappear"? If this case were being litigated in federal court, would the presumptions be treated any differently under FRE 301?

Chapter Thirty-Six

Judicial Notice

Focus on CEC 450–460

1. Judicial notice allows a fact to be deemed established with *no* evidence. Unlike a presumption, there is no predicate fact which has to be established. Judicial notice establishes a fact *conclusively*, so evidence cannot be offered to rebut it. If requested, the jury must be instructed that they must accept the fact which has been judicially noticed. CEC 457.

2. There are two forms of judicial notice under the California Evidence Code. Mandatory judicial notice is available for matters established by the constitution, statutes or rules of the State of California or the United States, the meaning of English words and phrases and all legal expressions, and facts that are "so universally known that they cannot reasonably be the subject of dispute." CEC 451. Mandatory means that, upon request, the court must take judicial notice of these facts. Discretionary judicial notice is available for the laws of other states, court records, facts that are of such "common knowledge" that they cannot reasonably be the subject of dispute, and facts that are capable of immediate and accurate determination by resort to sources of reasonable indisputable accuracy. CEC 452. A court must take discretionary judicial notice if a party gives sufficient notice of the request and furnishes the court with sufficient information to enable it to take judicial notice. CEC 453.

Judicial Notice Review Problem

The plaintiff sues for damages sustained when his automobile was rear-ended by the defendant's automobile in the inbound Harbor Freeway in Los Angeles at 5:30 a.m.

The defendant testifies that he was temporarily blinded when the sun got in his eyes, and that the distance between his car and the plaintiff's car in front of him was equal to the distance of a football field.

The plaintiff requests the court to take judicial notice of the following facts:

1. The Harbor Freeway in Los Angeles runs North and South, with the inbound lanes going North.
2. The sun rises in the East.
3. The Almanac reports that the sun rose at 6:02 a.m. on the date in question.

The defendant requests the court to take judicial notice that a football field is 100 yards long.

Would the court be required to take judicial notice of any of these facts pursuant to CEC 451? Pursuant to CEC 452?

Practice Transcripts

A. People v. Corleone
(Murder Conspiracy)

Don Vito Corleone is on trial for conspiracy to commit murder. The prosecution calls "Trigger Mike" Cerrina to testify that Corleone hired him as a "hit man" to murder 'Fat Frank" Fink, who Corleone suspected was a police informant. Cerrina was arrested on December 1, 2003, as he fled from a Los Angeles restaurant after shooting Fink six times. Fink miraculously survived, but lost his ability to speak due to a brain injury. Cerrina was given immunity in exchange for his testimony against Corleone. The following testimony is from the direct and cross examination of Cerrina at trial. Indicate the objections which Corleone's counsel would raise by writing the line number, then stating the grounds of the objection with citations to the California Evidence Code where appropriate. Give a full explanation of the probable ruling on the objection by the trial judge.

DIRECT EXAMINATION OF CERRINA:
1. Q. Are you acquainted with Tom Hagen?
2. A. Yes.
3. Q. How did you meet him?
4. A. I was introduced to Tom Hagen by Don Vito Corleone at Corleone's home in Beverly Hills on November 1, 2003.
5. Q. What did Corleone say when he introduced Hagen to you?
6. A. He said, "Mike, this is my consigliori, Tom Hagen. When Tom speaks, I speak, so listen to him very carefully."
7. Q. Were you familiar with the term "consigliori"?
8. A. Yes, that means a trusted advisor, sort of a right-hand man.
9. Q. When did you next hear from Tom Hagen?
10. A. Two weeks later he called me by telephone. I was at home in bed.
11. Q. What did he say?
12. A. He said, "Don Vito has a job for you. Fat Frank talks too much, and Don Vito wants him silenced permanently."
13. Q. What did you say?
14. A. I told him I'd take care of it right away, but I had to have $10,000 cash in advance.
15. Q. Did you receive the $10,000?
16. A. It was delivered to my home in a shoe box the next day. My wife told me Tom Hagen dropped it off.
17. Q. Then what did you do?

18. A. I started following Fat Frank around to see his pattern and plan the best way to kill him. I saw that he ate at Angelo's Restaurant every night, and I followed him there on December 1, 2003.
19. Q. Describe what happened that evening.
20. A. I had a loaded .45 automatic. I walked up to Fat Frank's table, pointed the gun at his face, spoke to him, and fired six times.
21. Q. What did you say before you fired the gun?
22. A. I said, "Don Vito sends his love."
23. Q. Did Fat Frank say anything in response?
24. A. Yes. He said, "Don Vito has me wrong. I've said nothing about him."
25. Q. What happened next?
26. A. After I emptied the gun, I ran for the door. I tripped over a chair an hit my head on a table. A bunch of people sat on me until the police came and arrested me.

CROSS EXAMINATION:
27. Q. After you were arrested, the police asked you if you knew Don Vito Corleone, didn't they?
28. A. I don't remember.
29. Q. Didn't you tell the police that you never heard of Don Vito Corleone?
30. A. I might have.
31. Q. Were you charged with attempted murder of Fat Frank Fink?
32. A. Yes.
33. Q. What happened to those charges?
34. A. They were dismissed when I agreed to testify before the grand jury last January.
35. Q. Weren't you also charged with the murder of Gino Galucci three years ago?
36. A. Yes, but those charges were dismissed for lack of evidence.
37. Q. Weren't you convicted of the murder of Jimmy Giulini twelve years ago?
38. A. Yes.
39. Q. How many murders have you committed?
40. A. I won't answer that.
41. Q. Isn't it true you've signed a contract to write a book and a movie script after this trial is over?
42. A. Yes.
43. Q. And that book will be called, "My Life As a Mafia Hit-Man"?
44. A. Something like that.
45. Q. When you testified before the grand jury in January, didn't you tell them you first met Tom Hagen at a party in Las Vegas?

46. A. Yes.
47. Q. Were you lying to the grand jury, or were you lying today in your direct testimony?
48. A. Neither.
49. Q. Did you report the $10,000 you received in the shoe box as income on your 2003 income tax return?
50. A. No.

B. Pringle v. Dimwit Dodge, Inc. (Negligent Entrustment)

On the evening of March 17, 2003, Paul Pringle was struck and injured by a hit-run driver as he walked across a cross-walk. A by-stander observed the accident, and described the car as a new Dodge Polara, license number DDD-013. The car was located the next morning, parked in front of Dimwit Dodge, Inc., a Dodge dealer. The car was owned by Dimwit Dodge, Inc., and was used as a "loan" car for customers whose auto was being repaired. Dennis Dimwit, owner and manager of Dimwit Dodge, denied that anyone had been given permission to use the car the night before., and claimed that the car had been stolen. Paul Pringle filed suit against Dimwit Dodge, Inc., alleging a single cause of action for "negligent entrustment". The complaint alleges that Dimwit Dodge, Inc., permitted Fred Fast, an employee, to drive the car, knowing he was a reckless driver. The jury will be given the following standard instruction from BAJI § 13.80:

> "In order to recover for negligent entrustment, the plaintiff must show (1) that reckless driving of an automobile owned by defendant caused the injuries to him; (2) that defendant permitted the driver to use this automobile; and (3) that defendant knew or should have known the driver was reckless or incompetent."

The following testimony is part of the direct examination of Fred Fast, who is called as a hostile witness by the plaintiff, and steadfastly denies that he was driving the Dodge Polara when it struck the plaintiff. Indicate the objections you would make if you were representing the defendant, Dimwit Dodge, Inc. Write the line number of the question or answer, and give a concise statement explaining the grounds of your objection, with citations to the California Evidence Code where appropriate. Then give a full explanation of the probable ruling of the trial judge.

1. Q. Where were you the night of March 17, 2003?
2. A. At a party at a friend's house.
3. Q. Have you ever borrowed a car for your own personal use from your employer, Dimwit Dodge?
4. A. Only once, in January of 2003.
5. Q. Were you involved in an accident with that car?

6. A. Yes, but it wasn't my fault. A tire blew.out and I hit a tree.
7. Q. Did you attempt to conceal that accident from your employer?
8. A. I took the car to another repair shop, hoping to get it fixed before I had to return it. But they called my boss, Mr. Dimwit, and he found out about the accident.
9. Q. What did Mr. Dimwit tell you when he found out about this accident?
10. A. He enclosed a note with my pay-check, which said if I ever did anything that stupid again, I could start looking for another job.
11. Q. Were you arrested at the time of this accident in January of 2003?
12. A. Yes.
13. Q. Were you given a test to determine your sobriety?
14. A. Yes, they gave me a breathalyzer test.
15. Q. Were you told the results of that test?
16. A. The cop said I blew a .12.
17. Q. Did you tell Mr. Dimwit about that?
18. A. No.
19. Q. How many times have you been arrested for drunk driving?
20. A. Four.
21. Q. Did you ever miss work because of these arrests?
22. A. Yes.
23. Q. Did you tell Mr. Dimwit why you missed work?
24. A. No, but he found out.
25. Q. How do you know he found out?
26. A. One of the secretaries told me Mr. Dimwit was complaining that every time he needed me, I was in jail on another drunk driving charge.
27. Q. On the morning of March 18, 2003, did you observe the Dodge Polara parked in front of Dimwit Dodge?
28. A. Yes, it was there when I arrived for work that morning.
29. Q. Did you inspect the car?
30. A. Yes. I noticed the keys were in the ignition, so I took them and put them in my pocket. And I saw the front end was a little smashed-up.
31. Q. Did you report this to anyone?
32. A. Yes, I told Mr. Dimwit when he came in.
33. Q. What did he do.
34. A. He called the police, and they came right away.
35. Q. Did any of the police officers speak to you?
36. A. Yes. Officer Wallace interviewed me.
37. Q. Did you tell Officer Wallace you had been home the entire previous evening?
38. A. I don't remember telling him that.

39.	Q.	Did you tell the Officer you had taken the keys out of the car that morning?
40.	A.	No, he didn't ask.
41.	Q.	What did you do with the keys?
42.	A.	I put them back on the rack in Mr. Dimwit's office.
43.	Q.	Incidentally, are the keys still kept on that rack in Mr. Dimwit's office?
44.	A.	No, after this all happened he started keeping them in his safe.
45.	Q.	Did you ask Officer Wallace whether the pedestrian who had been run down the night before was dead?
46.	A.	Yes.
47.	Q.	How did you know a pedestrian had been run down the night before?
48.	A.	I must have heard it on the radio.
49.	Q.	Did you discuss your testimony with the lawyer representing Dimwit Dodge before you came to court this morning?
50.	A.	Yes, he asked me to come to his office last night.
51.	Q.	Did he show you any documents?
52.	A.	Yes, we went over a memorandum he prepared describing the last time he interviewed me in Mr. Dimwit's office three years ago.
53.	Q.	Your Honor, I request that counsel for Dimwit Dodge provide me with that memorandum at this time.
54.	A.	THE COURT: We'll consider that request during the recess. Are you through with this witness?
55.	Q.	Just a couple more questions. Mr. Fast, isn't it true that you were hired by Dimwit Dodge because Mr. Dimwit owed a favor to your father, who happens to be his bookmaker?
56.	A.	I wouldn't know about that.
57.	Q.	Are you the same Fred Fast who was convicted of the felony of conspiracy to engage in bookmaking in Los Angeles County in 1976?
58.	A.	Yes.
59.	Q.	And wasn't your father one of the co-conspirators who was convicted with you?
60.	A.	Yes, but he was innocent.

C. People v. Rick E. Pugnant (Child Molestation)

Mr. and Mrs. Rick E. Pugnant own and operate the "Tiny Tots" Pre-School Center in Van Nuys, California. Rick has been charged with sexually abusing Victoria Voll, a four year old girl, who was left in the care of the "Tiny Tots" Pre-School Center by her mother on October 12, 2003. At his felony trial in the Superior Court for Los Angeles County, the prosecutor will present the testimony of three witnesses: Cheryl Voll, the sister of Victoria Voll; Mrs. Pugnant, the defendant's wife and co-owner of "Tiny Tots", and Dr. Ellen Eckhardt, a child psychologist. You are representing the defendant, Rick E. Pugnant. Indicate the objections you would make to the testimony offered by the prosecution at his trial. Write the line number of the question or answer, and give an explanation of the grounds of your objection, with citations to the California Evidence Code where appropriate.

Then give a full explanation of the probable ruling of the trial judge.

A. DIRECT EXAMINATION OF CHERYL VOLL:
1. Q. How old are you?
2. A. I'm eight years old.
3. Q. Are you related to Victoria Voll?
4. A. Yes, she's my sister.
5. Q. And how old is Victoria?
6. A. She's four and a half.
7. Q. Where did Victoria go to school last October?
8. A. She went to the "Tiny Tots" Pre-School
9. Q. Did you ever go to that school?
10. A. Yes, I went there too, before I started kindergarten.
11. Q. When was that?
12. A. Three years ago.
13. Q. Do you know Mr. Rick Pugnant, the man who's sitting at the table over there?
14. A. Yes, he was my teacher at "Tiny Tots".
15. Q. When Rick was your teacher, did he ever tell you to take your clothes off?
16. A. Yes. He played a game with me called "Lady Godiva". He told me to take all my clothes off, and then he would ride me around on his back like a horsey.

17. Q. Did you ever tell your mother about this game?
18. A. No.
19. Q. Why not?
20. A. Rick told me if I told anyone I couldn't play with the rabbit anymore.
21. Q. Did your sister, Victoria, ever tell you Rick played games with her?
22. A. Yes.
23. Q. What did she say?
24. A. She said Rick made her take off her clothes and play funny games with him.
25. Q. What did you do when your sister told you this
26. A. I told my mom right away.

DIRECT EXAMINATION OF MRS. PUGNANT:
27. Q. What is your occupation?
28. A. I am co-owner of the "Tiny Tots" Pre-School Center, which I operate in partnership with my husband, Rick.
29. Q. Was Victoria Voll enrolled at "Tiny Tots" in October of 2003?
30. A. Yes.
31. Q. Was she left alone with your husband, Rick, at any time in October, 2003?
32. A. Yes. On October 12, I received a call from Victoria's mother, who said she couldn't pick Victoria up until 7:00 p.m., which is an hour after we close. I had to run some errands, so I asked Rick if he could watch Victoria until her mother came.
33. Q. Were you present when Victoria's mother picked her up that day?
34. A. Yes, I got back at the same time Victoria's mother arrived.
35. Q. Did you hear Rick say anything to Victoria?
36. A. Yes, as he waved good-bye to her he said, "Don't forget what I told you about the rabbit."
37. Q. Did you ask him about that statement?
38. A. I don't remember
39. Q. Do you remember being interviewed by Sgt. Simon of the L.A.P.D. Child Abuse Detail on October 16, 2003?
40. A. Yes.
41. Q. Did you tell Sgt. Simon that you asked Rick what he told Victoria about the rabbit, and Rick said he and Victoria had a "special secret"?
42. A. Yes, I guess that's what I said.

DIRECT EXAMINATION OF DR. ELLEN ECKHARDT:
[Assume that an adequate foundation has been laid to qualify Dr. Eckhardt as an expert in child psychology].

43.	Q.	Did you examine Victoria Voll on October 15, 1983?
44.	A.	Yes.
45.	Q.	Please describe your examination.
46.	A.	I gave Victoria two anatomically correct dolls, one male and one female. Both were fully clothed. I said, "Let's pretend these dolls are Rick and you." I then observed her play with the dolls.
47.	Q.	Why was this procedure used?
48.	A.	Young children who are the victims of sexual abuse are often afraid to describe what happened to them. Through "play therapy", they will act out what happened to them with complete accuracy.
49.	Q.	What did Victoria do with the dolls?
50.	A.	She removed all of the clothing from both dolls, then placed the female doll on the back of the male doll, with legs astride as if riding a horse.
51.	Q.	Did you examine the results of the psychological profile tests administered to Rick E. Pugnant?
52.	A.	Yes.
53.	Q.	What did those tests reveal about Mr. Pugnant's personality?
54.	A.	That he has a passive dependent personality with highly guarded and defensive tendencies.
55.	Q.	Are these personality traits common among men who sexually abuse children?
56.	A.	Yes. A recent study conducted by the UCLA Family Support Program for Sexually Abused Children disclosed that 85% of 200 fathers who sexually abused their children had the same personality profile as Mr. Pugnant.
57.	Q.	Based on your examination of Victorial Voll, and your analysis of the psychological profile tests administered to Mr. Pugnant, did you form an opinion whether Victoria Voll was sexually abused by Rick E. Pugnant?
58.	A.	Yes.
59.	Q.	What is that opinion?
60.	A.	In my opinion, Rick E. Pugnant sexually abused Victoria Voll.

D. People v. Angela Muerta (Hospital Murders)

Angela Muerta is a registered nurse who was employed for a one-month period in the cardiac care unit at Holy Sepulcher Hospital. Suspicion was focused on her when fourteen patients in the cardiac care unit died during a one-month period in April, 2003. Normally, the hospital lost an average of one patient a month in that unit. All of the patients died during Angela's evening duty shift. The bodies of the fourteen patients were exhumed, and autopsies disclosed traces of potassium chloride in three of the corpses. Angela has been charged with the murders of those three patients: Henry Adams, John Brockman, and Lucinda Cuthart.

The testimony in Lines 1–26 is an excerpt from the direct examination of Dr. Donald Demento, a board-certified cardiologist with fourteen years experience in the treatment of patients with heart disease, called by the prosecution. The testimony in Lines 27–52 is an excerpt from the direct examination of Angela Muerta. Indicate the objections you would make to Dr. Demento's testimony if you were representing the defendant, then indicate the objections you would make to Angela Muerta's testimony if you were representing the prosecution. Write the line number of the question or answer, and give an explanation of the grounds for your objection, with citations to the California Evidence Code were appropriate. Then give a full explanation of the probable ruling of the trial judge.

DIRECT EXAMINATION OF DR. DONALD DEMENTO:
[Assume that an adequate foundation has been laid to qualify Dr. Demento as an expert in cardiology.]

1. Q. Doctor, were you on duty at Holy Sepulcher Hospital on the evening of April 16, 2003?
2. A. Yes.
3. Q. Were you called to respond to a "Code Blue"?
4. A. Yes, I was paged to report to the cardiac care unit for a "Code Blue" at 7:15 p.m.
5. Q. What does "Code Blue" mean?
6. A. It means a patient has gone into cardiac arrest, and needs to be resuscitated.
7. Q. Please tell us what happened.
8. A. When I arrived at the cardiac unit, the nurses summoned me to the bed where Norman Nelson was, and told me he had stopped breath-

ing. I immediately intubated him, attached a respirator, and began electrical defibrillation to start his heart going again. Within a few seconds, his heart pattern returned to normal and he began to stabilize.
9. Q. Did you converse with Mr. Nelson?
10. A. Well, he couldn't speak because intubation means he had a breathing tube through his mouth. But I explained to him that his heart had stopped and we were able to revive him. I told him everything seemed to be fine, and he was going to be all right. He nodded his head that he understood.
11. Q. Did you examine his chart?
12. A. Yes, I checked to see whether his chart showed any medication being administered within the previous six hours, and there were no entries.
13. Q. Did you say anything else to Mr. Nelson?
14. A. Yes, I wanted to make absolutely sure, so I asked him if he had received any medicine within the past six hours. He nodded his head yes, and made a gesture indicating an injection in his right arm. I examined his arm and observed a needle mark.
15. Q. Did you ask him who administered the injection?
16. A. Yes, I gave him a pencil and piece of paper, and asked him to write down the name of the person who gave him the injection. He wrote the name "Angela" and handed me the paper.
17. Q. I'm handing you People's Exhibit Eleven for identification. Is that the paper Mr. Nelson handed you?
18. A. Yes, it is.
19. Your honor, I move Exhibit Eleven in evidence.
20. THE COURT: It will be admitted.
21. Q. Doctor, where is Norman Nelson now?
22. A. Well, he recovered and was discharged from the hospital a week later, but in May of 2003 he was struck by a truck and killed.
23. Q. Doctor, based on your treatment of Mr. Nelson and your examination of his chart and Exhibit Eleven, do you have an opinion as to the cause of the cardiac arrest he suffered on April 16, 2003?
24. A. Yes, I do.
25. Q. What is that opinion?
26. A. I believe his cardiac arrest was caused by an unauthorized injection of a toxic substance by Angela Muerta.

DIRECT EXAMINATION OF ANGELA MUERTA:
27. Q. Miss Muerta, how long have you been a nurse?
28. A. Fourteen years.

29. Q. And how many hospital cardiac care units have you worked in?
30. A. Six.
31. Q. And until this case, has anyone ever complained about the quality of the care you gave to your patients?
32. A. No.
33. Q. Are you acquainted with Dr. Donald Demento?
34. A. Yes.
35. Q. Do you have an opinion as to his competence as a cardiologist?
36. A. Yes. He's not very good. He's always giving oral orders to the nurses.
37. Q. Are you familiar with his reputation among the hospital staff?
38. A. Yes.
39. Q. What is his reputation?
40. A. He's always trying to talk every nurse in the hospital into going to bed.
41. Q. Has he ever made an indecent proposal to you?
42. A. Yes, and I told him to get lost.
43. Q. Did you give an injection to Norman Nelson on April 16, 2003?
44. A. No, I did not.
45. Q. Did you look at his chart to see if anyone else gave him an injection?
46. A. Yes; I was worried that there might be some trouble, so I made a Xerox copy of his chart and saved it. It shows Nurse Laura Loose gave him an injection of lidocaine at 6:45 p.m., on the oral order of Dr. Demento.
47. Q. Who is Laura Loose?
48. A. She's Dr. Demento's girlfriend.
49. Q. Did you bring the copy you made of that chart to court today?
50. A. Yes, here it is.
51. Your honor, I'd like to mark this as Defense Exhibit B, and offer it in evidence.
52. THE COURT: I'll reserve ruling on that until after our recess.

E. People v. Don Defiler (Drug Possession)

Don Defiler, who is black, is on trial for possession of marijuana with intent to distribute. The following excerpts are taken from the direct and cross examination of Officer Paul Pride, testifying for the prosecution, and the direct and cross examination of Anthony Adams, testifying for the defense. Indicate the objections that should be interposed by opposing counsel to the testimony, showing the appropriate line number. Summarize the arguments that would be made both to support and to counter the objections, and give the judge's probable ruling. Apply the California Evidence Code.

DIRECT EXAMINATION OF OFFICER PAUL PRIDE:
1. Q. State your name.
2. A. My name is Paul Pride.
3. Q. Your occupation?
4. A. I am an officer of the San Jose Police Department, assigned to the narcotics enforcement division.
5. Q. How long have you been so employed?
6. A. Eleven years.
7. Q. Did you participate in the arrest of Don Defiler on November 1, 2003?
8. A. Yes, I placed Mr. Defiler under arrest for possession of marijuana for sale on that date, at his residence at 975 Sixth Street in San Jose.
9. Q. Did you conduct a search of the premises before you arrested Mr. Defiler?
10. A. Yes, pursuant to a search warrant issued by Judge Cordell, my partner, Officer Albert Adler and I conducted a thorough search of the premises.
11. Q. What did you find?
12. A. I found a total of 16 ounces of marijuana, packaged in individual plastic bags of one ounce each, in a bedroom closet.
13. Q. How did you know it was marijuana?
14. A. From its appearance and its smell.
15. Q. What did you do with it?
16. A. I gave it to Officer Adler and he delivered it to our Criminalistics Laboratory.
17. Q. Did they test it?
18. A. Yes, they did, and their report confirmed that it was marijuana, and that it weighed 16 ounces.

19. Q. What else did your search turn up?
20. A. Officer Adler found a 375 magnum handgun in the bathroom, along with $400 in cash.
21. Q. Anything else?
22. A. I found a stash of photos depicting sexual activity by children under the bed. We turned that stuff over to the federal authorities.
23. Q. Was anyone else present on the premises during your search, besides Don Defiler?
24. A. Yes, there was a white woman there who said she was his wife.
25. Q. What did she say when you found the marijuana?
26. A. She got all excited and said to Don Defiler, "You stupid shit, I told you to get rid of that stuff two weeks ago."
27. Q. Did Don Defiler say anything in response?
28. A. He just shrugged his shoulders and looked up at the ceiling.
29. Q. Did anyone else visit the premises while you conducted your search?
30. A. Yes, while we were searching the bedrooms there was a loud knocking at the front door. I yelled "Who's there," and heard a voice respond, "It's Jeff. Tell Don I'm here for my stuff." When I opened the door, a young boy approximately fourteen years old ran from the scene.
31. Q. Did his statement have any special meaning to you?
32. A. In the drug culture, "stuff" is frequently used as a term for marijuana. I'm sure he was there to buy some marijuana from Don Defiler.
33. Q. Did Don Defiler say anything when you placed him under arrest?
34. A. Yes, he claimed the marijuana was for his own use for treatment of a medical condition, chronic back pain.
35. Q. Did you believe that?
36. A. No responsible doctor would recommend marijuana for back pain.
37. Q. Do you have an opinion whether this marijuana was possessed for purpose of distribution?
38. A. Yes. Based on the quantity, the means of packaging, as well as the large quantity of cash and a firearm, my opinion is that Don Defiler is a major dealer selling marijuana to kids in his neighborhood.

CROSS-EXAMINATION:
39. Q. Officer Pride, you've arrested Don Defiler before, haven't you?
40. A. Yes, this was the fourth time I've arrested him for dealing drugs.
41. Q. And on all three of the prior occasions, the charges were dismissed, weren't they?

42. A. Yes, because the evidence was suppressed.
43. Q. And on the last occasion, when charges were dismissed on April 18, 2002, did you say to Don Defiler, "We'll get you next time, you dumb nigger!"?
44. A. No, I never said that.
45. Q. Is it your testimony you never called Don Defiler a "nigger"?
46. A. I never use that word.
47. Q. Do you ever use racial epithets when you speak to arrested suspects?
48. A. No, that would be unprofessional.

DIRECT EXAMINATION OF DEFENSE WITNESS ANTHONY ADAMS:

49. Q. State your name.
50. A. My name is Anthony Adams.
51. Q. Mr. Adams, are you acquainted with Officer Paul Pride of the San Jose Police Department?
52. A. Yes, I am.
53. Q. How do you know him?
54. A. He arrested me four times, and he arrested lots of my friends, too.
55. Q. Did Officer Pride ever refer to your race when he arrested you?
56. A. The last time he arrested me, a year ago, he said "get your black ass in the back of that patrol car."
57. Q. Are you familiar with Officer Pride's reputation for racial hostility in the community?
58. A. Yes. All my friends say he's a racist.

CROSS-EXAMINATION:

59. Q. Is Don Defiler a friend of yours?
60. A. I know him, but we've never socialized.
61. Q. Have you done drugs together?
62. A. No.
63. Q. Are you the same Anthony Adams who was convicted of the felony of assaulting a police officer in San Jose on April 23, 1992?
64. A. Yes.
65. Q. And are you the same Anthony Adams who was convicted of misdemeanor possession of marijuana on June 11, 2002?
66. A. Yes.
67. Q. And was Officer Pride the one who arrested you on that charge?
68. A. Yes.

F. People v. Hart
(Murder by Poison)

Wilma Hart is on trial for the murder of her wealthy husband, Henry Hart, who died of cyanide poisoning on the evening of November 13, 2003, after consuming a cookie baked by Wilma. The cookie contained large quantities of cyanide derived from the kernels of peach pits. Wilma's defense is that the death was accidental. The following transcript presents excerpts from the testimony of four witnesses: the paramedic who responded to a 911 call, called by the prosecution; a medical expert called by the prosecution; the defendant, testifying on her own behalf, and the defendant's current husband, called as a prosecution rebuttal witness. Applying the California Evidence Code, indicate the line number at which objections should have been interposed, explaining the grounds for the objections, the appropriate response, and the probable ruling of the trial judge.

DIRECT EXAMINATION OF ARNOLD ABLE:
1. Q. Did you respond to an emergency call in Los Gatos, California on the evening of November 13, 2003?
2. A. Yes, we received a call that a man was experiencing severe respiratory distress at 945 East Mountainside Road, and responded with red lights and siren in an emergency ambulance.
3. Q. Were you informed who made the emergency call?
4. A. Yes, I was told by the dispatcher that the man's wife made a 911 call and she said he had a bad heart condition and was having a heart attack.
5. Q. Describe what happened when you arrived at the premises.
6. A. We arrived at 8:14 p.m. The man was lying on his back on the dining room floor. He was clutching his throat and gasping for air. As I prepared to give him oxygen, he spoke in a hoarse whisper.
7. Q. What did he say?
8. A. He said, "Laughed when I fell. Cookie tasted weird. I think Wilma poisoned me."
9. Q. Were you able to revive him?
10. A. No, the oxygen did not seem to help, and he went into cardiac arrest and died in the ambulance on the way to the hospital.
11. Q. Did you inform Wilma Hart of her husband's death?
12. A. Yes, she followed our ambulance to the hospital. After he was pronounced dead in the emergency room, I informed her of his death, and told her an autopsy would have to be performed.

13. Q. What was her response?
14. A. She seemed more upset about the autopsy than anything else. She insisted that there was no need for an autopsy, since it was so obvious he died of a heart attack.
15. Q. Can you identify People's Exhibit No. 1?
16. A. Yes, this is a partially eaten cookie which was lying beside Mr. Hart's body when we arrived at the premises. I retrieved it, placed it in this plastic bag, and brought it with us to the hospital for toxicological testing.
17. Q. Did the defendant indicate any concern about your taking the cookie?
18. A. Yes, she tried to grab it away from me. She said, "why are you taking that? If you're hungry, I'll get you a sandwich." I told her we might have to test it. She said, "I ate one too, and I'm just fine."

CROSS-EXAMINATION:
19. Q. When the defendant told you it was obvious her husband died of a heart attack, did she say anything else?
20. A. Yes, she said he had been complaining of pains in his chest for two weeks, but she couldn't convince him to see a doctor.
21. Q. Are you aware that the defendant consented to a complete search of her home after the autopsy, and that she allowed the police to seize all of the uneaten food in the house?
22. A. Yes, I read about that in the newspapers.
23. Q. Were you interviewed by newspaper reporters about the death of Mr. Hart?
24. A. Yes.
25. Q. And did you tell them you were absolutely convinced that Mrs. Hart was trying to "cover up" the full circumstances of her husband's death?
26. A. Yes, I did say that.

DIRECT EXAMINATION OF DR. BERNARD BAKER:
[Assume Dr. Baker has qualified as an expert in pathology and toxicology].
27. Q. Doctor, what documents and records did you consult in preparing for your testimony in this case?
28. A. I reviewed the autopsy report, the toxicology report, the transcripts of the coroner's hearing, and all medical files related to the deceased.
29. Q. Based on your examination of these records, do you have an opinion as to the cause of death of Henry Hart?

30. A. Yes, I have concluded he died of cyanide poisoning caused by the ingestion of a large concentration of crushed kernels of peach pits contained in a cookie he consumed shortly before he died.
31. Q. Do the symptoms of cyanide poisoning resemble a heart attack?
32. A. Yes. Claiming heart attack is a perfect way to conceal poisoning by cyanide.
33. Q. Did you find any evidence that Henry Hart had any history of a heart condition?
34. A. No. His medical records and the autopsy report suggest he was in perfect health, with no signs or symptoms of any difficulty with his heart.
35. Q. In your opinion, could this have been an accidental poisoning?
36. A. No. Based upon the quantity of poison and the circumstances of its administration, I believe this was a deliberate murder.
37. Q. What circumstances convinced you that this was a deliberate murder?
38. A. Well, the toxicologist's report indicates that seven cookies were tested, and the only one containing cyanide was the one consumed by the deceased.
39. Q. Anything else?
40. A. Yes, the testimony at the coroner's hearing offered by the mother of the deceased suggests that there was a good deal of marital discord, and the deceased had threatened to divorce the defendant.

CROSS-EXAMINATION:
41. Q. Doctor, are you familiar with an article entitled "Accidental Poisoning By Cyanide," by Doctor Herman Goering, which appears in the International Journal of Toxicology for August, 1973?
42. A. Yes, but that's quite outdated, and I did not consider it or rely upon it in this case.
43. Q. But isn't Dr. Goering recognized as the leading authority in the entire world on cyanide poisoning?
44. A. Yes, he seems to be obsessed by cyanide. Probably has something to do with his uncle's death.
45. Q. Do you disagree with Dr. Goering's conclusion that there is remarkable disparity in the concentration of cyanide between the pits of peaches grown in Africa, and those grown in North America?
46. A. Yes, I think Goering's right about that. African peaches have much higher concentrations of cyanide.
47. Q. Were you able to ascertain the origin of the peach-pit kernels that were contained in the cookie consumed by Henry Hart?

48. A. The toxicology report did not indicate that, but I read somewhere that African peach-pit kernels are red, while those from North America are brown. The cookie crumbs looked brown to me.

DIRECT EXAMINATION OF DEFENDANT WILMA HART:
49. Q. Were you aware that the cookie you served your husband contained the kernels of peach pits?
50. A. No. It was made with ground almonds.
51. Q. Where did you acquire the ground almonds?
52. A. From a health food store. The package was labeled "imported from Africa."
53. Q. Did you deliberately poison your husband?
54. A. No. I loved him very much, and was devastated by losing him.

CROSS-EXAMINATION:
55. Q. How much do you expect to inherit from your husband's estate?
56. A. His net worth was approximately $8 million, and he had $2 million worth of life insurance naming me as the beneficiary.
57. Q. Henry Hart was not your first husband, was he?
58. A. No. I was married twice before.
59. Q. And your first husband died of an accidental overdose of drugs?
60. A. That's correct. He was a heavy drinker, and took too many sleeping pills. That was fifteen years ago.
61. Q. How much did you inherit when he died?
62. A. Barely enough to bury him.
63. Q. And your second husband died an accidental death as well?
64. A. He fell off a steep cliff six years ago.
65. Q. And you were standing next to him when he slipped and fell?
66. A. Yes.
67. Q. How much did you inherit when he died?
68. A. He left an estate of less than $500,000.00
69. Q. When did you first learn that the kernels of peach pits contain cyanide?
70. A. I did not know that until they explained to me the cause of my husband's death.
71. Q. You recently remarried for a fourth time, is that correct?
72. A. Yes, I married Mr. Don Defiler in May of this year.
73. Q. When were you charged with the murder of Henry Hart?
74. A. On April 10, 2004.
75. Q. And is it true you and Mr. Defiler were having an illicit affair at the time Henry Hart was poisoned?

76. A. No, that is not true.
77. Q. Have you ever been convicted of a felony?
78. A. Yes. Eight years ago, my second husband was convicted of tax fraud for not reporting income from the sale of real estate. Since I signed the tax return, I was convicted along with him. We both received probationary sentences.

DIRECT EXAMINATION OF DON DEFILER:
79. Q. Are you currently married to Wilma Hart?
80. A. Yes.
81. Q. When were you married?
82. A. On May 30, 2004.
83. Q. Did you carry on an affair with Wilma Hart while she was married to Henry Hart?
84. A. I decline to answer that.

G. People v. Dowling (Spousal Murder)

Defendant Howard Dowling is on trial for the murder of his wife, Wanda, who died of a shotgun wound in the back while standing at the sink in the family kitchen on March 1, 2001. Howard told police that the shotgun discharged accidentally while he was cleaning it, seated at the kitchen table. The prosecution case included the testimony of Wanda's twenty-five year old daughter by a previous marriage, Debra Dowling, and the grand jury testimony of Sheila Strong, a woman who was a close friend of both Wanda and Howard, then subsequently married Howard. In Howard's defense, he presented the testimony of Ben Bradley, a friend and hunting companion, and Edward Elder, a firearms expert. The following transcript presents excerpts from the testimony of these four witnesses. Applying the California Evidence Code, indicate the line number at which objections should have been interposed, explaining the grounds for the objections, the appropriate response, and the probable ruling of the trial judge.

DIRECT EXAMINATION OF DEBRA DOWLING:
1. Q. What is your relationship to the defendant?
2. A. I was adopted by him after he married my mother when I was nine years old.
3. Q. Prior to her death, did your mother tell you her future plans?
4. A. Yes, one month before her death, she told me she was going to leave Howard, because he had become abusive and was carrying on with another woman.
5. Q. Did your mother keep a diary?
6. A. Yes, she showed me where she kept it, under her mattress.
7. Q. Did you ever read her diary?
8. A. Yes, two weeks before she died, I was house-sitting while she and Howard were out of town, and I did read her diary, because I was worried about the things she had told me about Howard.
9. Q. Were you able to locate her diary after her death?
10. A. No. I looked under her mattress and it was gone. I asked Howard whether he had taken it, and he just smiled and shrugged his shoulders.
11. Q. Did the diary describe the infliction of any physical injuries upon your mother?
12. A. Yes. She described three occasions during the previous month when Howard and she had loud arguments, ending by Howard striking her

with his fists. She wrote that on each of these occasions, Howard threatened to kill her if she left him.

CROSS-EXAMINATION:
13. Q. What is the value of your mother's estate?
14. A. About four million dollars.
15. Q. If Howard is convicted of murder in this case, all that money will go to you, is that correct?
16. A. I don't really know, and I don't really care.
17. Q. Have you retained a lawyer to challenge Howard's right to inherit under your mother's will?
18. A. Yes.
19. Q. You hate Howard Dowling, don't you?
20. A. He murdered my mother.
21. Q. Haven't you always resented his relationship with your mother?
22. A. No.
23. Q. Didn't you move out of the family home as soon as you turned eighteen?
24. A. Yes.
25. Q. And did you tell your mother you refused to live under the same roof as Howard?
26. A. Yes.

RE-DIRECT EXAMINATION:
27. Q. Can you tell us why you refused to live in the same house with the defendant?
28. A. He tried to molest me when I was thirteen years old.
29. Q. Did you ever tell anyone about that?
30. A. No, I was afraid of him.

GRAND JURY TESTIMONY OF SHEILA STRONG:
The prosecution called Sheila Strong as a witness. She declined to testify, on the grounds that she married the defendant on July 1, 2003, three months after giving testimony before the grand jury. The trial judge overruled her claim of privilege, relying on Section 972 (f) of the California Evidence Code, and ordered her to testify. She refused to do so, and was held in contempt of court. The prosecutor was then permitted to read the following testimony presented under oath to the grand jury by Sheila Strong on April 1, 2003:

31. The Court: Ladies and gentlemen of the jury: Sheila Strong, who is now married to the defendant, has defied the order of this court to testify in these proceedings and was held in contempt of court. Be-

cause she is unavailable to testify, the testimony she gave to the grand jury in this case will now be read to you. You may proceed.

32. Q. Did Wanda Dowling tell you she was planning to leave Howard?
33. A. Yes, around Christmas time last year, she said she suspected Howard was seeing another woman, and said she was going to see a lawyer about a divorce.
34. Q. In fact, you knew Howard was having an affair with another woman, didn't you?
35. A. Yes.
36. Q. Because you were the woman he was having an affair with, weren't you?
37. A. Yes.
38. Q. Did you tell Wanda you were having an affair with her husband?
39. A. Of course not.
40. Q. Did you tell Howard what Wanda had said?
41. A. Yes. About a week later.
42. Q. How did he respond?
43. A. He said, "Don't worry about Wanda. I'll take care of her."
44. Q. And did your affair with Howard continue?
45. A. No. I told Howard we should stop seeing each other. I did not want to be in the middle of a messy divorce.

DIRECT EXAMINATION OF BEN BRADLEY FOR THE DEFENSE:
46. Q. Did you accompany Howard Dowling on a hunting trip in February of 1999?
47. A. Yes, we went deer hunting over the President's Day weekend.
48. Q. What weapon did he bring?
49. A. He brought his Remington G-2 shotgun.
50. Q. Did his shotgun accidentally discharge at any time?
51. A. Yes. We were stalking a deer when his shotgun discharged into a tree.
52. Q. Did Howard say anything when this happened?
53. A. Yes, he said he wasn't even touching the trigger. He said "the damn thing went off when I brushed against the hammer." He said it probably needs a good cleaning.
54. Q. Did you ever talk to Howard about the circumstances of his wife's death?
55. A. Yes. Two days after it happened, he told me, "The damn thing went off while I was cleaning it, just like on our hunting trip. I didn't even know it was loaded."
56. Q. Do you have an opinion about Howard Dowling's character for peacefulness and non-violence?

57. A. Yes. Howard is a good Christian and a very peaceable man. He would never hurt anyone. He was devastated by the accidental death of his wife. He loved her very much.

CROSS-EXAMINATION:

58. Q. Did you know that Howard Dowling struck his wife with his fists on at least three occasions during the month preceding her death?
59. A. No. I find that hard to believe.
60. Q. Are you the same Ben Bradley who was convicted of misdemeanor larceny for shoplifting cigars from the San Jose Smoke Shop in July of last year?
61. A. Yes, but it was all a misunderstanding. I forgot I had them when I left the shop.
62. Q. Weren't they concealed in your underwear?
63. A. That's how I always carry my cigars.
64. Q. Did Officer Smith of the San Jose Police Department ask to interview you about Howard Dowling last April?
65. A. Yes.
66. Q. And did you refuse to speak with him?
67. A. I just told him I was too busy to meet with him at that time.

DIRECT EXAMINATION OF EDWARD ELDER:

68. Q. Please describe your training in the examination and repair of firearms.
69. A. For thirty years, until I retired, I was the director of quality control for the Remington Firearms Manufacturing Company. My job was to direct the final inspection of all firearms before they were shipped, and to investigate all complaints of defects in our products. Since my retirement six years ago, I have operated a gun repair shop.
70. Q. Are you familiar with the Remington G-2 shotgun?
71. A. Yes, I have inspected hundreds of those, and repaired at least fifty of them.
72. Q. Did you examine the Remington G-2 shotgun that killed Wanda Dowling?
73. A. Yes, I did.
74. Q. Did you discover any defect that could cause the gun to discharge accidentally while being cleaned?
75. A. Yes. On this particular weapon, the pin that holds the hammer became dislodged, and brushing against the hammer can cause it to discharge.
76. Q. Do you have an opinion as to whether Howard Dowling murdered his wife, Wanda?

77. A.   Yes. In my opinion he did not deliberately kill her. It was an accident.

CROSS-EXAMINATION:

78. Q.   Are you being paid for your testimony today?
79. A.   Yes, I'm charging my normal rate for forensic work of $250 per hour.
80. Q.   In your opinion, if one were aware that a weapon had accidentally discharged, would he not check to make absolutely sure the weapon was not loaded before attempting to clean or repair it?
81. A.   That would certainly be the most prudent course.
82. Q.   And if one were aware that a weapon had accidentally discharged, would he point it at his wife's back while cleaning or repairing it?
83. A.   That would not seem prudent.
84. Q.   Are you familiar with the instruction manual for the Remington G-2 shotgun?
85. A.   Yes, I am.
86. Q.   What does the manual say about repairing or cleaning this weapon?
87. A.   It says one should always unload the weapon before attempting to repair or clean it, and the weapon should never be pointed at another person while repairing or cleaning.

H. Pringle v. Thomas & Neeley (Sexual Harassment)

Plaintiff Paula Pringle is suing the San Francisco law firm of Thomas & Neeley, where she was employed as a paralegal, for sexual harassment and wrongful discharge. She alleges that senior partner Floyd Neeley, to whom she was assigned to provide litigation support, frequently grabbed her breasts and buttocks, and left indecent proposals on her e-mail. She complained to managing partner Andre Thomas, who took no action for a month, then after she continued to complain, demanded that she take a polygraph test. Polygraph tests were administered to Ms. Pringle and Mr. Neeley and the test administrator concluded both were deceptive. Ms. Pringle was then fired. After she filed this lawsuit, Mr. Neeley jumped from the 15th story window of his law office and died.

The following transcript presents excerpts from the direct and cross examination of Andre Thomas, Paula Pringle, and Edwin Ellis, the polygraph operator. Applying the California Evidence Code, indicate the line number at which objections should have been interposed, fully explaining the grounds for the objections, the appropriate responses, and the probable ruling of the trial judge.

DIRECT EXAMINATION OF ANDRE THOMAS:
1. Q. Did you serve as managing partner at the law firm of Thomas & Neeley?
2. A. Yes, from January 1, 1992 until the present.
3. Q. During that period, did Ms. Pringle complain to you that Floyd Neeley was harassing her?
4. A. Yes. She first told me on April 11, 2003, that Mr. Neeley had placed his hands on her breasts without her permission, and that he put his hand up her dress on several occasions.
5. Q. Did you subsequently discuss this matter with Mr. Neeley?
6. A. Yes, I saw him in his office the next day and asked him about it.
7. Q. What did he say?
8. A. He said Paula had come on to him and that they engaged in "heavy petting" with her consent. He was very embarrassed, and assured me it wouldn't happen again.
9. Q. Did you then discuss the matter with Ms. Pringle?
10. A. Yes. She accused him of lying and kept complaining to me that we were "covering it up." I didn't know who to believe. I finally asked them both to take a lie detector examination.

11. Q. Did you subsequently discharge Ms. Pringle?
12. A. Yes, when the polygraph results showed she was lying, I fired her.
13. Q. When you say you didn't know who to believe, did you have any reason to disbelieve Ms. Pringle?
14. A. Yes. She had a reputation in the firm for exaggerating. I was also aware that she had engaged in "heavy petting" with other employees of the firm.
15. Q. How did you become aware of that?
16. A. I heard one of the file clerks boasting at the office Christmas party.

CROSS-EXAMINATION:
17. Q. Were you present on the day of Mr. Neeley's death in July of 2003?
18. A. Yes. I was immediately called by a secretary who saw him climb out the window of his office.
19. Q. Do you believe he committed suicide?
20. A. Yes, he even left a note, which I found on his desk.
21. Q. What did the note say?
22. A. It said, "I can't take any more of Paula's lies. She destroyed everything I have to live for. I'm going to end it all."
23. Q. Was he despondent?
24. A. Yes, he really went into a tailspin over the charges Ms. Pringle made against him.
25. Q. Were you aware of Mr. Neeley's reputation in the community for honesty?
26. A. Yes. It was superb. He was widely respected for his honesty. He was a man of his word.

RE-DIRECT EXAMINATION:
27. Q. Was Mr. Neeley ever accused of harassing any other employees?
28. A. Well, ten years ago his secretary quit. She claimed he couldn't keep his hands off of her, but Floyd said she was angry over not getting a bonus.
29. Q. Have you heard that Mr. Neeley was held in contempt of court in 1996 for concealing relevant evidence in discovery proceedings?
30. A. Yes. The judge later rescinded her order, however, when Floyd explained that a paralegal had misfiled the evidence.

DIRECT EXAMINATION OF PAULA PRINGLE:
31. Q. Did you ever indicate to Mr. Neeley that you consented to his sexual touchings?
32. A. No. I repeatedly pushed his hands away and asked him to stop.
33. Q. Did he send you indecent proposals via the office e-mail?

34. A. Yes. On April 9, 2003, I received an e-mail message from him that said I should take off my panties before I come into his office.
35. Q. After you complained to Mr. Thomas, did Mr. Neeley say anything to you?
36. A. Yes. The day after I complained, he came to my office and said Andre told him I was complaining about him. He said if I kept complaining I would get myself fired. He said he didn't understand why I was so upset over a little touching. He said, "I didn't even get into your pants. If I'd known you were such a prude, I wouldn't have come near you."
37. Q. Did he say anything else?
38. A. Yes, he said none of the other girls ever complained.
39. Q. Were you aware that he fondled any other female employees?
40. A. Yes. Two of the other paralegals told me he had grabbed them in a sexual way.
41. Q. Do you have an opinion as to the honesty of Andre Thomas?
42. A. Yes. I think he's a liar who would say anything to protect the reputation of his law firm.

CROSS-EXAMINATION:
43. Q. When you first complained to Mr. Thomas on April 11, 2003, did you tell him about the e-mail?
44. A. No.
45. Q. In fact, you sent that message to yourself, using Mr. Neeley's computer, didn't you?
46. A. Absolutely not.
47. Q. Were you aware that a paralegal received a $1 million judgement against another San Francisco law firm for sexual harassment in March of 2003?
48. A. Yes, I read about it in the newspaper.
49. Q. Did that give you the idea that you could collect a lot of money by accusing Mr. Neeley of sexual harassment?
50. A. Absolutely not.
51. Q. Did you tell Nora Jamison on April 16, 2003, that you finally found a way to become a millionaire?
52. A. No, that's a lie.

DIRECT EXAMINATION OF EDWIN ELLIS:
53. Q. What is your occupation?
54. A. I am a professional polygraph operator, employed by a national firm of employment security consultants since 1995.
55. Q. Please describe your background and training.

56. A. I received my training in use of the polygraph at the FBI Academy in Quantico, Virginia. I did polygraph testing for the FBI for twenty years, up until my retirement in 1995. I have written several books and numerous papers on the reliability of polygraph examinations, and served as President of the National Association of Polygraph Examiners in 1997. I am also a deacon in the Methodist Church.

57. Q. Is the reliability of polygraph testing generally accepted in the field of employment security?

58. A. Yes, the federal government has used it for 30 years to make decisions about the hiring and firing of its employees. Nearly every large employer in America has relied upon polygraph results to resolve employment disputes.

59. Q. Did you conduct a polygraph examination of Paula Pringle in late April of 2003?

60. A. Yes, I did.

61. Q. Did you do any investigation prior to conducting that examination?

62. A. Yes. I interviewed several employees at the law firm of Thomas & Neeley. I learned that an indecent e-mail message was found on Ms. Pringle's computer, that it came from Mr. Neeley's computer, and that at the date and time it was sent, Mr. Neeley was not in the office. I also spoke to a secretary in the office named Nora Jamison, who told me Ms. Pringle had bragged to her about finding a way to become a millionaire.

63. Q. Did you ask Ms. Pringle about the e-mail message during the polygraph examination?

64. A. Yes. She claimed it was from Mr. Neeley.

65. Q. Based on your examination of the polygraph results, did you form an opinion whether that answer was truthful?

66. A. Yes. In my opinion, her answer to that question was highly deceptive.

67. Q. Did you ask her whether she boasted to Ms. Jamison about finding a way to become a millionaire?

68. A. Yes. She denied making such a statement.

69. Q. Based on your examination of the polygraph results, did you form an opinion whether that answer was truthful?

70. A. Yes. In my opinion, she was lying when she denied making that statement.

CROSS-EXAMINATION:

71. Q. Did you ask Ms. Pringle whether Floyd Neeley put his hand up her dress?

72. A. Yes. She said he had.

73. Q. Did you ask her whether she consented to Floyd Neeley's sexual touching?
74. A. Yes. She said she did not.
75. Q. Were her responses to these questions truthful?
76. A. Yes. In my opinion, they were.
77. Q. Did you conduct a polygraph examination of Mr. Neeley?
78. A. Yes, I did.
79. Q. Were any of his answers deceptive?
80. A. In my opinion, he was truthful in saying he believed Ms. Pringle consented to his advances, but when I asked him if he ever asked her to remove any clothing, his answers were deceptive. I concluded that he probably went further with her than he was willing to admit, and that she planted the e-mail message to strengthen her case against him.
81. Q. Did you advise the law firm of Thomas & Neeley to fire Ms. Pringle?
82. A. No, I actually recommended they reach a settlement with her.
83. Q. Was your retirement from the F.B.I. voluntary?
84. A. Yes.
85. Q. Were you under investigation for falsifying requests for overtime payments at the time you resigned?
86. A. Yes, but those charges were false.

J. Price v. Ford Motor Co. (Wrongful Death)

Plaintiff Pearl Price is suing the Ford Motor Co. for wrongful death of her husband John, who died when his 2001 Lincoln convertible left the road and collided with a tree. The Plaintiff contends the collision was caused by a failure in the power steering mechanism attributable to a design defect. The Defendant contends Mr. Price was driving under the influence of alcohol and missed a turn in the road.

The following transcript presents excerpts from the direct and cross-examination of Pearl Price, Deputy Sheriff Alan Lane, and Dr. Edward Ellis. Applying the California Evidence Code, indicate the line number at which objections should have been interposed, fully explaining the grounds for the objections, the appropriate responses, and the probable ruling of the trial judge.

DIRECT EXAMINATION OF PEARL PRICE:
1. Q. Did your husband John ever tell you he was having problems with his 2001 Lincoln?
2. A. Yes. A week before he died, he said he was going to call the dealer and arrange to take the car in, because it was getting harder to steer.
3. Q. What did you say?
4. A. I told him he should call right away, that he shouldn't be driving the car if there's something wrong with the steering. He said he'd take care of it right away.
5. Q. Was John a safe driver?
6. A. Oh yes, he always buckled up and never went over the speed limit.
7. Q. Did he ever drink and drive?
8. A. Oh, he would often have a glass of beer or wine with dinner, but he wouldn't get drunk, if that's what you mean.
9. Q. On the night of the collision, do you know where John had been that evening?
10. A. He had been on a business trip to Los Angeles. He called home around 7 p.m. and said he would be late because he was stopping to visit his mother at the nursing home. He said he would stop for a bite to eat on the road.

CROSS-EXAMINATION:
11. Q. This was not the first time Mr. Price ran his car off the road, was it?

12. A. No, he had a small accident in 2000 and a bad one in 1997.
13. Q. The "small accident" was when he hit a kid on a bike?
14. A. Yes, the child was not seriously injured, though.
15. Q. And Mr. Price was cited for reckless driving?
16. A. Yes.
17. Q. And the bad accident was when he fell asleep at the wheel?
18. A. Yes, he had been driving straight home from a business trip to Las Vegas.
19. Q. And was he charged with driving under the influence of alcohol on that occasion?
20. A. That charge was dropped when he pled guilty to reckless driving.
21. Q. Was that a plea bargain deal?
22. A. I really don't know what it was.
23. Q. Did Mr. Price have automobile insurance?
24. A. Yes.
25. Q. And did he have life insurance?
26. A. Yes.
27. Q. And how much have you already collected on those insurance policies?
28. A. $500,000.
29. Q. When Mr. Price called to tell you he was coming home late, did he sound tired?
30. A. Not really.
31. Q. Did you testify at a deposition for this case on July 21, 2003 at the law office of your attorney?
32. A. Yes.
33. Q. And did you give the following testimony under oath: "John called around 7 and said he had a rough day and was anxious to get some sleep when he got home."
34. A. Yes. But he didn't sound particularly tired.
35. Q. Did he complain at all about any problems with the steering of his car?
36. A. No.

DIRECT EXAMINATION OF DEPUTY SHERIFF ALAN LANE:
37. Q. Did you respond to a radio report of a collision on Highway 485 near Lancaster on March 20, 2003 at 11 p.m.?
38. A. Yes, I did.
39. Q. Please describe what you observed.
40. A. On a Northbound stretch of 485, where the highway turns west, I found a 2001 Lincoln convertible had left the road and collided with a large Monterey Pine tree.
41. Q. Was anyone in the automobile when you arrived?

42.	A.	The driver was pinned behind the wheel, very badly injured. He had lost a lot of blood.
43.	Q.	Was he conscious?
44.	A.	I saw his eyes blink and he was groaning. I told him an ambulance was on the way.
45.	Q.	Did he say anything?
46.	A.	He said "I think I can make it. My steering wheel went out." I tried to get him out, but he died from massive internal bleeding before the ambulance arrived.
47.	Q.	Did you examine the highway for skid marks?
48.	A.	There were none. It looked like he just kept heading due north, left the highway and plowed into the tree.
49.	Q.	How fast was his car traveling?
50.	A.	The speed limit is 60 m.p.h., but from the front of his car I'd say he was driving 80.
51.	Q.	Were there any witnesses at the scene?
52.	A.	A lady had pulled over and reported the accident on her cell phone. She waited twelve minutes until I got there. She said she was right behind him, and he drove right off the road. She never even saw his brake lights light up.

CROSS-EXAMINATION:

53.	Q.	Did you prepare a report on this case?
54.	A.	Yes, I did after I received the coroner's report two days after the accident.
55.	Q.	And was this report done within the scope of your duties as a deputy sheriff?
56.	A.	Yes, it was.

The following report was then admitted in evidence.

"On March 7, 2003, at 11 p.m., Mr. John Price was killed when his 2001 Lincoln convertible left northbound Highway 485 and collided with a tree. Before his death, Mr. Price attributed the collision to a steering failure. Subsequent blood alcohol tests revealed he had a blood alcohol level of .09%. Mrs. Stephanie Worth was behind Mr. Price's vehicle and reported that his car was weaving. She thought he was drunk or fell asleep and drove off the road."

DIRECT EXAMINATION OF DR. EDWARD ELLIS:

[Assume Dr. Ellis has been qualified as an expert in automobile accident reconstruction].

| 57. | Q. | Did you examine the power steering mechanism for the 2001 Lincoln in which Mr. Price died? |

58. A. Yes, I disassembled the mechanism at the garage to which the vehicle was towed after the collision, on March 28, 2003.
59. Q. What did you find?
60. A. I discovered that premature wear on the rubber fittings caused leakage of the power steering fluid, which then caused failure of the power steering system.
61. Q. Is wear on these fittings normal?
62. A. One might expect the fittings to wear out after many years, but this car was only two years old. The fittings were made with a very cheap grade of rubber.
63. Q. Has premature wear of the power steering fittings caused other accidents in 2001 Lincolns?
64. A. Yes, I am aware of three other accidents caused by premature wear on these fittings, all during the year 2002.
65. Q. Has Ford Motor Co. made any effort to replace these fittings?
66. A. Yes, they issued a recall in February of 2004 to replace the power steering fittings in all 2001 Lincolns.
67. Q. How much did Ford save by using a cheaper grade of rubber for these fittings?
68. A. They saved about fifteen cents per fitting.

CROSS-EXAMINATION:
69. Q. Dr. Ellis, you never visited the actual scene of the accident, did you?
70. A. No, I was not retained until several weeks after the accident occurred.
71. Q. How much power steering fluid does the 2001 Lincoln power steering mechanism hold?
72. A. Approximately 14 ounces.
73. Q. Were you aware that 12 ounces of power steering fluid were recovered in a puddle at the accident scene?
74. A. No, I was not.
75. Q. Would that change your opinion as to the cause of the accident?
76. A. That would depend on where it was found, and how it was measured.
77. Q. In how many cases have you testified as an expert for the plaintiff?
78. A. Approximately two hundred.
79. Q. Ever testified for the defense?
80. A. No.
81. Q. And you're paid well for your testimony, aren't you? How much are you getting for this one?
82. A. Eight thousand dollars.
83. Q. For six hours?

84. A. I don't charge by the hour.
85. Q. Do you advertise your services in lawyer's magazines?
86. A. Only in one publication of the American Trial Lawyer's Association.
87. Q. And in that advertisement, do you boast that you have testified "successfully" in two hundred cases?
88. A. Yes.
89. Q. What does "successfully" mean?
90. A. That I was qualified as an expert.
91. Q. In your report for this case, did you state that the power steering mechanism had already been disassembled when you examined it?
92. A. I don't recall what it says in my report. The mechanism had previously been examined by other experts, but they put it back together.
93. Q. Is this your report?
94. A. Yes.
95. Q. I request this be marked as Defense Exhibit 6, admitted in evidence, and shown to the jury.
96. Q. Did you testify as an expert in the case of Flowers v. Ford Motor Co. in 1999?
97. A. Yes, I did.
98. Q. And in that case, the jury rejected your testimony and found for the defendant, didn't they?
99. A. They did.

K. People v. Scott (Spousal Murder)

Defendant Peter Scott is on trial for the murder of his pregnant wife Stacy and the fetus she was carrying. Stacy Scott disappeared from the home she shared with Peter on Christmas Eve, 2003. Her body and the remains of her fetus were discovered two miles north of the Berkeley Marina four months later. Peter's defense is that he left to go fishing at the Berkeley Marina the morning of Christmas Eve, and when he returned home Stacy was missing.

The following fictional transcript presents excerpts from the direct and cross-examination of five witnesses: Mrs. Mary Moore (Stacy's Mother); Mrs. Nora Neely (who lived next door to Peter and Stacy Scott); Julie Jones (a massage therapist whom Peter was seeing), Dr. Edwin Ellery, an expert retained by the defense, and the defendant, Peter Scott. Applying the California Evidence Code, indicate the line number at which objections should be interposed, fully explaining the grounds for the objection, the appropriate responses, and the probable ruling of the trial judge. Any resemblance to actual persons or cases is coincidental.

DIRECT EXAMINATION OF MRS. MARY MOORE:
1. Q. When was the last time you spoke to your daughter?
2. A. The evening of December 23, she called around 9 p.m.
3. Q. What did she say?
4. A. She asked what she could bring for our family dinner Christmas Eve. She said she and Peter would come around 6 p.m.
5. Q. Did she tell you anything about her plans for the next day?
6. A. She said she had all her Christmas shopping done, she just needed to pick up a few things at the grocery store.
7. Q. Did she say anything at all about Peter going fishing?
8. A. No, she did not mention that at all.
9. Q. When did you learn that Stacy was missing?
10. A. Peter called an hour before they were due to come for dinner, and said he could not find Stacy and the dog was missing. He said he had gone fishing that day by himself. I was surprised by that, because I'm sure Stacy would have told me if a fishing trip was planned.
11. Q. During their five years of marriage, did Stacy ever complain to you that Peter struck her or abused her?
12. A. I now recall one occasion, about a month before he killed her. She had a black eye. She joked about walking into a door, but later when

we were alone she said Peter "lost his temper" when they were arguing, and hit her with his fist.

CROSS-EXAMINATION:
13. Q. Mrs. Moore, did you give a statement to Officer Wallace of the Oakland Police Department when police were investigating your daughter's disappearance in January of this year?
14. A. Yes, I did.
15. Q. And did you tell Officer Wallace that you had no knowledge of any arguments or disagreements between Peter and Stacy Scott?
16. A. Yes, but I had forgotten the black eye incident.
17. Q. When did you remember that incident for the first time?
18. A. When I read in the newspaper that he gave his girl-friend a black eye, then I remembered he did the same thing to Stacy.

DIRECT EXAMINATION OF MRS. NORA NEELY:
19. Q. Did you observe Peter Scott at any time on the morning of December 24, 2003?
20. A. Yes. I was looking out my kitchen window and saw him loading stuff into the back of his truck.
21. Q. Did you see any of the items he was loading?
22. A. Well, there was something wrapped up in a huge blue tarp. It was almost six feet long and about two feet wide. He carried it over his shoulder and laid it in the truck bed.
23. Q. Do you have an opinion whether Peter Scott is a violent person?
24. A. Yes, I think he is a violent person with a very bad temper.
25. Q. Did you ever observe him engage in any violence directed toward his wife Stacy?
26. A. Well, I never saw him hit her, but once I saw him beating her dog with a stick, and she became very upset about it.
27. Q. In your opinion, what was in the tarp that you saw Peter place in his truck?
28. A. I think it was the body of Stacy Scott.

CROSS-EXAMINATION:
29. Q. Mrs. Neely, were you convicted of shoplifting at a Pic' N Save store in July of 1998?
30. A. Yes, I was.
31. Q. Have you ever told anyone that you would "do everything you could" to see that Peter Scott got the death penalty?
32. A. I don't recall saying anything like that.

33. Q. Do you deny that on April 19 of this year, after Stacy's body was found, you said to Mrs. Bridget Spellicy, quote, I'm going to do everything I can to see that bastard is executed for this, unquote.
34. A. Yes, I deny that. Bridget Spellicy is looney if she says that.

DIRECT EXAMINATION OF JULIE JONES:
35. Q. How did you meet Peter Scott?
36. A. He started coming to my office for weekly massages in August of 2003.
37. Q. Did you then start dating him?
38. A. Yes, we started seeing each other on a regular basis, every weekend, starting in September.
39. Q. Did he tell you he was married?
40. A. No, he told me he had been divorced and was single.
41. Q. Did he ever ask you to marry him?
42. A. Not directly, but several times he said he was ready to settle down, and talked about what a "sweet wife" I would be.
43. Q. Did he ever strike you?
44. A. Yes, on two occasions. Both times he had too much to drink and lost his temper. In early October, we had an argument and he hit me with his fist and gave me a black eye. I told him we were through, but he sent flowers and candy and was so apologetic, I said I'd give him another chance. Then in late November he became very jealous about my having dinner with another client and he slapped me.
45. Q. When did you learn that Peter Scott was married?
46. A. After his wife disappeared and there was so much publicity about it, I saw him on television and recognized him.
47. Q. Did you speak with him again after that?
48. A. He called me in early January, and said it was very important that I "keep quiet" about our relationship. He said he couldn't see me for a while, but after this was "all over" he wanted to get back together, because he said he still loved me. I told him I was really upset that he lied to me about being single. He said, "Well now I am."

CROSS-EXAMINATION:
49. Q. Have you had "dating" relationships with other clients of your massage service?
50. A. Yes.
51. Q. What proportion of your massage clients are men?
52. A. All of them.
53. Q. How much was Peter Scott paying you for his massages?

54. A. $100 per session is my standard rate.
55. Q. And did he continue to pay for his weekly massages throughout your relationship?
56. A. Well, he owed me quite a bit toward the end. He didn't always pay right away.
57. Q. Have you ever been arrested for soliciting prostitution?
58. A. Three arrests, but I've never been convicted.
59. Q. Were you interviewed on television about your relationship with Peter Scott?
60. A. Yes.
61. Q. Were you upset about the publicity about your relationship?
62. A. Yes.
63. Q. Are you acquainted with Ms. Angela Allenby?
64. A. Yes, Angie does my nails.
65. Q. Did you tell Ms. Allenby "All this publicity has really been great for my business. I have more customers that I've ever had before?"
66. A. I might have said something like that.

DIRECT EXAMINATION OF DR. EDWIN ELLERY:
[Assume that Dr. Ellery has been qualified as an expert in Marine Biology and Oceanography].

67. Q. Have you studied the water currents and marine life in San Francisco Bay?
68. A. For over thirty years.
69. Q. Do you have an opinion as to when the body of Stacy Scott was placed in the waters of San Francisco Bay?
70. A. Yes. In my opinion the body was in the water no more than thirty days when it was found.
71. Q. On what do you base that opinion?
72. A. On the condition of the body, the degree of deterioration, the condition of the water, the weather conditions, and the location where the body was found.
73. Q. And do you have an opinion where the body of Stacy Scott was placed in the water?
74. A. Yes. In my opinion it was dropped from the San Rafael Bridge, thirty miles from where it was found.
75. Q. Did you conduct an experiment to verify your conclusions?
76. A. Yes. I dropped the carcass of a dead sheep wrapped in a tarp from the San Rafael Bridge on May 1. Thirty days later, it washed up near the Berkeley Marina.

CROSS-EXAMINATION:

77. Q. How much are you being paid for your work as an expert witness in this case?
78. A. I am billing at my customary rate of $350 per hour. Thus far, I have devoted 200 hours to this case, for a total of $70,000.
79. Q. Are you familiar with the work of Dr. Alonzo Hartley on the deterioration of human bodies submerged in water for long periods of time?
80. A. I have read his work, but do not consider it authoritative.
81. Q. Are you aware that he has succeeded in the identification of human remains in sunken ships that have been submerged as long as fourteen years?
82. A. No.
83. Q. Do you disagree with his conclusion, stated in the April, 1992 issue of the Journal of Forensic Science, that the conditions of San Francisco Bay are ideal for the preservation of submerged human remains?
84. A. I think that research is out-dated. Pollution of the Bay in the past twelve years has increased the acidity of the water.
85. Q. In 1987, were you dismissed from a position as research director for the United States Oceanographic Survey?
86. A. I resigned from that position.
87. Q. And was your resignation related to the discovery that survey data had been falsified?
88. A. Allegations of falsified data were never proven.
89. Q. If, as you believe, Stacy Scott's body was placed in the waters of San Francisco Bay thirty days prior to its discovery, do you have any idea how long she was already dead before her body was placed in the water?
90. A. No, I don't believe that can be ascertained from the information available.

DIRECT EXAMINATION OF DEFENDANT PETER SCOTT:

91. Q. Did you murder your wife Stacy and unborn child?
92. A. Absolutely not.
93. Q. Did you ever strike your wife?
94. A. No.
95. Q. Did you load anything wrapped in a tarp into your truck on the morning of December 24?
96. A. No. On December 21, I returned some large rented lawn umbrellas, and loaded them into the truck. Mrs. Neely may have confused what she saw on December 21 with December 24.

97. Q. Did you get a receipt for the return of the umbrellas?
98. A. Yes, and it's dated December 21.
99. Q. Do you have an opinion whether Mrs. Neely is an honest person?
100. A. Yes. In my opinion she is a liar who can't be trusted. On several occasions she spread false rumors about other people in the neighborhood. She's just a busybody who likes to stick her nose in everyone's business and gossip about them.
101. Q. Were you having an affair with Julie Jones?
102. A. Not really. I was using and paying for her services as a prostitute.

CROSS-EXAMINATION:
103. Q. Did you take out a $500,000 life insurance policy on the life of your wife Stacy?
104. A. Yes, with the baby coming we thought we should have insurance.
105. Q. How often did you go on fishing trips alone?
106. A. A couple times a month. I like to fish.
107. Q. When you spent week-ends with Julie Jones, how did you explain those trips to your wife?
108. A. I told her I was going fishing.
109. Q. So you lied to your wife?
110. A. Yes.
111. Q. You lied to the police after your wife disappeared too, didn't you?
112. A. No.
113. Q. Didn't you tell Officer Olson that you were not having relationships with any other women?
114. A. Yes, but I didn't really consider my use of Julie's services as a "relationship."
115. Q. How frequently did you use the services of prostitutes during your marriage to Stacy?
116. A. Four or five times.
117. Have you ever made threats against any of the prostitutes whose services you used?
118. A. No.
119. Q. Do you deny that on August 17, 1998, you told Agnes O'Halloran that you would strangle her with your bare hands if she did not leave your apartment?
120. A. That was before I married Stacy. Agnes was trying to get more money than we agreed upon.

L. People v. Defiler
(Rape)

Don Defiler is an all-star center for an N.B.A. basketball team. On September 14, 2003, he was checking in to the Silverado Resort in Napa, California. The resort assigned Vivian Vilna to show him around the resort, a special service provided to V.I.P. guests. When she escorted him to his room, he embraced her and began removing her clothing. She now claims that despite her protests, he forced her to submit to both vaginal and anal intercourse. He has been charged with violations of Sections 261 and 286 of the California Penal Code. Section 261 provides:
"Rape is an act of sexual intercourse accomplished with a person not the spouse of the perpetrator…where it is accomplished against a person's will by means of force, violence, duress, menace, or fear of immediate and unlawful bodily injury on the person or another." Section 286 provides:
"Sodomy is sexual conduct consisting of contact between the penis of one person and the anus of another person. Any sexual penetration, however slight, is sufficient to complete the crime of sodomy.… Any person who commits an act of sodomy when the act is accomplished against the victim's will by means of force, violence, duress, menace, or fear of immediate and unlawful bodily injury on the victim or another person shall be punished…" Defiler admits having vaginal intercourse, but claims that Vivian consented. He denies that he engaged in any act of anal intercourse with her. The following fictional transcript presents excerpts from the direct and cross-examination of six witnesses: Vivian Vilna; Dr. Rex Morgan, who examined her after the alleged rape; Ellen Jones, an expert on Rape Trauma Syndrome testifying for the prosecution; Felicity Forest; Nathan Hooper, a team-mate testifying for the defense; and Don Defiler. Applying the California Evidence Code, indicate the line number at which objections should be made, fully explaining the grounds for the objection, the appropriate responses, and the probable ruling of the trial judge.

DIRECT EXAMINATION OF VIVIAN VILNA:
1. Q. Please describe what happened after you escorted Mr. Defiler to his room.
2. A. He shut the door and grabbed me around the waist and started unbuttoning my blouse. I told him to stop but he wouldn't. He removed my clothing and pushed me over a chair and raped me from behind, and then he sodomized me.

3. Q. Did you say or do anything to indicate you were consenting to sexual intercourse or sodomy with Mr. Defiler?
4. A. No, I protested throughout, and was crying. I told him he should be ashamed of himself.
5. Q. Did he say anything in response?
6. A. He just rolled his eyes, and said, "I thought you came with the room."
7. Q. Did you tell him you were going to file a rape complaint?
8. A. Yes.
9. Q. Did he say anything in response?
10. A. He said, "I'm sorry if I hurt you. I'll pay for any treatment you need. I'll give you as much as you want. I just don't want my wife to find out about this."

CROSS-EXAMINATION:
11. Q. Are you acquainted with Mr. Defiler's team-mate, Nathan Hooper?
12. A. Yes.
13. Q. Did you escort Mr. Hooper around the hotel two weeks prior to Mr. Defiler's visit?
14. A. Yes.
15. Q. Did you have consensual sexual intercourse with Mr. Hooper?
16. A. Yes.
17. Q. Did Mr. Hooper tell you he would recommend you to his team-mates?
18. A. He said he would tell his team-mates what a great resort we had.
19. Q. In fact, before you escorted Mr. Defiler to his room, did he tell you that Mr. Hooper had told him about you?
20. A. Yes.
21. Q. You did not report this incident to the police until two days after it occurred, did you?
22. A. No. I was very embarrassed by it, and didn't go to the police until my mother insisted I report it.
23. Q. And when did you tell your mother about this?
24. A. I told her about it the next morning after it happened.
25. Q. And when you reported it to the police, you said you had been raped, but you made no mention of any anal intercourse, is that correct?
26. A. Yes, I was too embarrassed. No one had ever done that to me before.
27. Q. When did you first tell anyone that Mr. Defiler had also sodomized you?
28. A. I told the Doctor at the hospital when he examined me.

DIRECT EXAMINATION OF DR. REX MORGAN:
29. Q. Were you the physician in charge of the emergency room at St. Barthlomew Hospital on September 16, 2003?

30. A. Yes.
31. Q. Did you examine Ms. Vilna?
32. A. I did not examine her myself, but I reviewed the examination report by Dr. Helen Horowitz, the admitting physician.
33. Q. What did Dr. Horowitz's examination disclose?
34. A. She reported that the vaginal area was normal, with no apparent trauma, but there was bruising and abrasions in the area surrounding the victim's anus.
35. Q. Did you ask Ms. Vilma how these injuries were sustained?
36. A. Yes. She said she had been raped and sodomized by Don Defiler two days earlier.

CROSS-EXAMINATION:

37. Q. Did Ms. Vilna appear embarrassed or reluctant to tell you she had been sodomized?
38. A. She seemed embarrassed by the entire examination. I didn't note any greater embarrassment over the sodomy than over the rape.
39. Q. If both acts were perpetrated by force, what explanation would there be for the absence of bruises or abrasions in the area of the vagina?
40. A. She may have resisted the anal intercourse more vigorously than the vaginal intercourse; or the perpetrator may have exerted greater force to accomplish the anal intercourse.
41. Q. Did you inquire whether Ms. Vilna had engaged in sexual activity with others besides Don Defiler within the previous week?
42. A. Yes.
43. Q. What did she tell you?
44. A. She told me she had intercourse with her boyfriend the night before the examination, but she said had never had anal intercourse before she was sodomized by Don Defiler.

DIRECT EXAMINATION OF ELLEN JONES:

45. Q. Please describe your background and training.
46. A. I have been the Director of the Napa County Rape Crisis Center for ten years. I provide training in what is commonly called the Rape Trauma Syndrome for Napa County law enforcement agencies. I am certified as a Rape Crisis Counselor by the State of California, and have a Masters Degree in Psychology. Over the course of the past ten years, I have counseled over one thousand victims of sexual assaults, and testified as an expert on Rape Trauma Syndrome thirty times.
47. Q. Did you provide counseling to Vivian Vilna, the victim in this case?
48. A. Yes, I have met with Ms. Vilna six times in the past three months.

49. Q. In your opinion, is she experiencing the Rape Trauma Syndrome?
50. A. Yes, I believe she is.
51. Q. Please explain what the Rape Trauma Syndrome is?
52. A. Rape Trauma Syndrome is a cluster of behaviors common to victims of sexual assaults. The syndrome was identified in a study conducted in 1973 by Ann Burgess and Linda Holstrom, in which they identified recurring patterns of activity in hundreds of victims. The study has been replicated many times since with the same results. A common defense mechanism for victims of sexual assaults is denial, by minimizing the ordeal they have experienced. As many as 90% of rapes are never reported. They may delay reporting the crime, and when they do report it, they often make incomplete or selective disclosure of the details.
53. Q. Is it likely, for example, that a victim who had been both raped and sodomized would report only the rape to the police?
54. A. That would be a very common response for a victim afflicted with Rape Trauma Syndrome.
55. Q. Did Ms. Vilna tell you that Don Defiler had forced her to submit to both vaginal and anal intercourse?
56. A. Yes, she did.
57. Q. And did she explain why she did not report the anal intercourse to the police?
58. A. Yes, she was especially embarrassed about that, and she told me no one had ever had anal intercourse with her until Don Defiler sodomized her.

CROSS-EXAMINATION:
59. Q. Do you believe that all accusations of rape are truthful?
60. A. No.
61. Q. Do you believe you have some special talent to determine which accusations are truthful and which are not?
62. A. I can only deal with probabilities, and the presence of symptoms of the Rape Trauma Syndrome make it more likely that a victim is telling the truth.
63. Q. Are you familiar with the critique of the Burgess & Holstrom study published by Dr. Aaron Feldman in Psychology Today for May of 1997?
64. A. I've heard about it, but never read it.
65. Q. Do you disagree with Dr. Feldman's observation that Burgess and Holstrom assumed that all of the victims they examined were truthful without any corroborating evidence?
66. A. I do disagree with that.

DIRECT EXAMINATION OF FELICITY FOREST:
67. Q. What is your occupation?
68. A. I am employed as a maid at the Ritz-Carlton Hotel in New York.
69. Q. Do you know Don Defiler?
70. A. Yes, unfortunately. I was assigned as the maid for a room he occupied at the Ritz Carlton in August of 1997.
71. Q. Did Mr. Defiler force you to submit to any sexual contact with him on that occasion?
72. A. Yes. He came into the room while I was making it up. He embraced me and began removing my clothes. I told him to leave me alone. He then tore off my clothing and forced me to submit to sexual intercourse with him. Then he forced me to submit to anal intercourse as well.

CROSS-EXAMINATION:
73. Q. When is the first time you reported to anyone that Don Defiler had raped you?
74. A. When I saw on television that he was accused of raping another woman just like he raped me.
75. Q. So you waited six years without ever telling anyone?
76. A. Yes.
77. Q. As a result of your testimony in this case, you have received lots of media attention, haven't you?
78. A. I've been interviewed a couple times, and appeared on some talk shows.
79. Q. And you came to New York to be an actress, didn't you?
80. A. Yes, I work as a maid between acting jobs.
81. Q. Members of Mr. Defiler's basketball team are frequent guests at your hotel, are they not?
82. A. Yes.
83. Q. And have you engaged in sexual activity with other members of Mr. Defiler's team?
84. A. I decline to answer that on the grounds my answer may tend to incriminate me.

DIRECT EXAMINATION OF NATHAN HOOPER FOR THE DEFENSE:
85. Q. Were you a guest at the Silverado Resort in August of 2003?
86. A. Yes.
87. Q. Did you meet Vivian Vilna at that time?
88. A. Yes, she escorted me around the resort when I arrived.
89. Q. Did you have sexual relations with her?
90. A. Yes. After she showed me around we went back to my room and partied and had sex.

91. Q. Did you engage in anal intercourse with her?
92. A. Yes.
93. Q. Did you tell Don Defiler about your having sexual relations with Ms. Vilna?
94. A. Yes, I told him all about her.
95. Q. Are you also acquainted with Felicity Forest?
96. A. Yes.
97. Q. Have you had sexual relations with her?
98. A. Yes, she parties with the team whenever we stay at the Ritz-Carlton in New York.
99. Q. Do you have an opinion as to her character for honesty?
100. A. Yes. I do not think she is an honest person. She would say anything to get her name in the papers.

DIRECT EXAMINATION OF DEFENDANT DON DEFILER:
101. Q. Did you rape Vivian Vilna?
102. A. I did not. She consented to having sexual intercourse with me.
103. Q. Did you force her to engage in anal intercourse with you?
104. A. Absolutely not. We did not have anal intercourse.
105. Q. Did you rape Felicity Forest?
106. A. Absolutely not. She consented to having sexual intercourse with me on numerous occasions.

CROSS-EXAMINATION:
107. Q. Were you convicted of a misdemeanor offense of shop-lifting in Los Angeles in 1994?
108. A. Yes.
109. Q. And in 1998, were you suspended from participation in N.B.A. games for thirty days, for the use of steroid drugs?
110. A. Yes.

Objections to Transcripts

[ALL REFERENCES TO TEXT ARE TO **CHAPTER:NUMBERED PARAGRAPH**].

A. People v. Corleone

5. Hearsay. Overruled: Party admission, offered against Corleone by prosecution. [**Text 20:1**]. It can also be argued that Coreleone's words conferring authority on Hagen have an independent operative effect. [**Text 19:4**].
7. Improper opinion. Sustained: No foundation to qualify witness as an expert to explain terms. [**Text 29:3**].
9. Lack of authentication. Sustained: Cerrina has not testified how he knew it was Hagen calling. [**Text 30:1**].
11. Hearsay. Overruled: Authorized admission [**Text 20:3**] or Co-conspirator statement. [**Text 20:5**].
13. Hearsay. Overruled: To show effect on listener. [**Text 19:4**].
14. Hearsay ("My wife told me"). Sustained.
21. Hearsay. Overruled: Co-conspirator statement. [**Text 20:5**].
23. Hearsay. Overruled: Spontaneous statement [**Text 23:1**] or state of mind [**Text 23:4**].
29. Hearsay. Overruled: Prior inconsistency. [**Text 21:1**].
31. Improper character evidence, no conviction. Overruled: offered to show bias. [**Text 15:4**].
35. Improper character evidence, no conviction. Sustained: Prop. 8 permits specific instances, but only if relevant to truthfulness. [**Text 15:1**].
37. Improper character evidence. Sustained. Conviction relates to moral turpitude, but is remote. [**Text 15:7**].
39. Improper character evidence, irrelevant. Sustained: Only convictions or specific instances related to truthfulness permitted. [**Text 15:1**]. If overruled, witness must invoke privilege to refuse testifying.
41. Irrelevant. Overruled: Admissible to show bias. [**Text 15:4**].
45. Hearsay. Overruled: Prior inconsistency. [**Text 21:1**].
47. Argumentative. Sustained. [**Text 32:11**].
49. Irrelevant, Improper character evidence. Overruled: Specific instance permitted under Prop. 8, is relevant to truthfulness. [**Text 15:3**]. May also be relevant to show bias, if he is not being prosecuted for tax evasion because he is testifying.

B. Pringle v. Dimwit Dodge

5. Relevancy. Overruled: Prior accident used to show propensity for negligence. Responses: not offered to prove negligence, but to prove knowledge of employer. [Text 10:6].
7. Relevancy. Overruled: Evidence of specific act of bad character (concealment) to show propensity or to attack credibility. Response: offered to prove knowledge of employer. [Text 10:6].
8. "They called my boss." Move to strike: No personal knowledge, hearsay. Sustained: Lack of personal knowledge. [Text 18:3].
8. Hearsay. Overruled: Admission of party. Relevant to show knowledge. [Text 20:1].
10. Secondary Evidence. Where is the note? Sustained. [Text 31:2].
11. Relevancy. Sustained: Inadmissible bad character evidence, not relevant to prove knowledge of employer. [Text 10:6].
15. Hearsay. Sustained.
19. Relevancy. Improper character evidence. Sustained. [Text 10:6].
26. Double hearsay. Sustained: Statement of Dimwit is admission, but Statement of Secretary would not qualify as agent's statement or authorized admission. [Text 20:3].
31. Hearsay. Overruled: Not offered to prove truth, but show knowledge of listener. [Text 19:4].
39. Relevancy. Overruled: Use of silence as prior inconsistency or concealment. Was it an assertion?
43. Subsequent remedial measure. Sustained. [Text 6:1].
45. Hearsay. Overruled: Not offered to prove truth, but to show prior knowledge of declarant. [Text 19:4].
53. Right to see material used to refresh recollection. Sustained. [Text 22:2]. No Attorney-client privilege. [Text 34:5].
55. Relevancy. 352. Sustained. [Text 4:4].
57. Impeachment by felony. Admissible under *Beagle?* [Text 15:6].
60. Relevancy. 352. Sustained. [Text 4:4].

C. People v. Pugnant

15. Relevancy. 352. Overruled: Prior bad act admissible for propensity. (Cheryl is not the victim in this trial.) [Text 11:1]. Common scheme? [Text 10:1].
17. Hearsay. Overruled: Not assertion. Not to show truth. [Text 19:5].

20. Hearsay. Overruled: Party Admission. [**Text 20:1**].
21. Hearsay. Sustained. No exception available.
25. Hearsay. Sustained: Prior consistency offered before any inconsistency offered. [**Text 21:5**].
27. Spousal privilege. Sustained: She can assert privilege not to testify against her spouse. [**Text 33:10**].
32. Lack of authentication of source of phone call. Sustained. [**Text 30.1**]. Hearsay—Victoria's mother. Overruled: Offered to show effect on the listener. [**Text 19:4**]. Hearsay—"I asked Rick." Overruled: Offered to show effect on listener. [**Text 19:4**]. Privilege for marital communication?
35. Hearsay. Overruled: Party Admission. [**Text 20:1**]. Not marital communication.
39. Hearsay. Overruled: Prior inconsistency. Is claimed memory loss genuine? [**Text 21:4**]. Rick's statement is admission.
43. Assert Kelly-Frye objection. Although she is qualified expert, no showing "play therapy" is generally accepted in scientific community. [**Text 29:4**].
49. Hearsay. Assertive conduct? Reasonably relied upon by expert? [**Text 29:5**].
51. Hearsay. Overruled: Use by expert. [**Text 29:5**].
53. Secondary Evidence. Sustained. [**Text 31:2**].
56. Relevancy. Propensity of bad character? 352. [**Text 4:7**].
60. Improper opinion. Sustained: Beyond expertise. [**Text 29:2**].

D. People v. Angela Muerta

9. Relevancy. Improper character evidence. Overruled: Norman Nelson is not one of the victims charged. Admissible to prove identity of perpetrator, based on similarity of incidents. [**Text 10:3**].
10. Hearsay (Dr. Demento's statements to Nelson). Overruled: Offered to show effect on listener. [**Text 19:4**].
12. Hearsay. Overruled: No foundation to show chart is business record. But no intended assertion; in any event absence of entry would be admissible under Section 1272. [**Text 24:6**]. Secondary evidence. Sustained: Where is the chart? [**Text 37:2**].
14. Hearsay. Assertions intended by gestures. Probably sustained: No medical diagnosis exception available. Section 1251 not available. [**Text 23:7**]. Dying declaration? Told he would be all right. Subsequently recovered. [**Text 25:5**].
16. Hearsay. Sustained: Identification? He did not testify. [**Text 21:7**]. Dying declaration? Told he would be all right. [**Text 25:5**].

22. Hearsay. Sustained: No showing of personal knowledge. [**Text 18:3**].
26. Improper opinion. Sustained: Who gave injection is beyond his expertise. [**Text 29:6**].
31. Relevancy. Good character? What trait? [**Text 12:2**]. Hearsay. Absence of complaints as implied assertions? [**Text 19:5**].
35. Qualifications to give expert opinion not shown. Sustained. [**Text 29:3**]. Bad character evidence? Only truthfulness is relevant. [**Text 15:1**]. Offered to show relevant habit? [**Text 14:5**].
37. Relevancy. Improper character evidence. Sustained: Only his reputation for honesty is relevant. [**Text 15:1**].
41. Relevancy. Overruled: Admissible to show bias. [**Text 15:4**].
46. Hearsay? Secondary evidence? (This is the problem portrayed in *The Verdict*). [**Text 31:5**].

E. People v. Don Defiler

13. No foundation for opinion. Must be qualified as expert. [**Text 29:3**].
18. Hearsay, Secondary Evidence. Sustained: No foundation for Official Record exception. [**Text 24:4**]. No explanation where report is. [**Text 31:2**].
20. Relevancy. 352. [**Text 4:1**].
22. Relevancy. 352. Probably sustained: objection much stronger re: danger of prejudice. [**Text 4:1**].
26. Hearsay. Overruled: Not offered for truth, but for effect on listener. [**Text 19:4**]. Excited Utterance exception. [**Text 23:1**].
28. Hearsay. Overruled: Party Admission. Implied assertion from silence. [**Text 19:5, 20:1**].
30. Hearsay. Overruled: Not offered to prove truth of statement, but to infer nature of premises from knowledge of declarant. [**Text 19:4**]. Relevancy?
32. No foundation for opinion. Sustained. [**Text 29:3**].
34. Hearsay. Overruled: Party Admission. [**Text 20:1**].
36. Improper opinion; not qualified as expert. Sustained. [**Text 29:3**].
38. Opinion goes beyond expertise. [**Text 29:6**].
40. Improper character evidence. Overruled: Arrests not admissible to show bad character, but here they are offered by defense to show bias. Limiting instruction should be requested. [**Text 15:4**].
43. Relevancy. 352. Hearsay. Overruled: Relevant to show bias and motive. [**Text 15:4**]. Not hearsay because offered to show state of mind of declarant. [**Text 19:4**].
56. Relevancy. Sustained: This does not rebut Pride's testimony.

58. Hearsay. Relevancy. Only reputation for honesty is admissible under Section 786. Does Prop.8 make this admissible? [Text 15:1].
63. Relevancy. 352. Assault not related to honesty. [Text 15:7]. Ten years old. But may be admissible to show bias. [Text 15:4].
65. Relevancy. 352. Conviction is misdemeanor. [Text 15:7]. But may also be admissible to show bias. [Text 15:4].

F. People v. Wilma Hart

4. Double hearsay. Overruled: Wife to dispatcher—admission. [Text 20:1]. Dispatcher to Able—not to prove truth, but to show effect on listener. [Text 19:4].
7. Hearsay. Dying Declaration? No personal knowledge. [Text 25:5]. Excited Utterance? [Text 23:1].
13. Hearsay. Overruled: Admission. [Text 20:1].
17. Hearsay. Overruled: Admission [Text 20:1], State of Mind of declarant [Text 19:4].
19. Hearsay. Not admission when offered by defendant on cross-examination. Is it admissible to "complete" under Section 356? [Text 20:1].
22. No personal knowledge. Sustained. [Text 18:3].
25. Relevancy. To show bias? [Text 15:4]. Hearsay. To show state of mind of speaker? [Text 19:4].
32. Non-responsive. Motion to strike prejudicial portion. 352. [Text 4:1]
33. Limiting Instruction. Sources ordinarily relied upon by experts. [Text 29:5].
36. Opinion beyond expertise. [Text 29:6].
40. Hearsay of mother. Not ordinarily relied upon by experts. [Text 29:5].
45. Hearsay. Not considered or relied upon by expert. But did he admit it was reliable authority, per Section 721? [Text 29:7].
48. Relevancy. Sustained. Color of crumbs does not prove color of kernels. [Text 2:1].
52. Hearsay, Secondary Evidence. Where is package? [Text 31:2].
55. Relevancy. Overruled: To show bias and motive. [Text 2:1, 8:1].
59. Relevancy, 352. To show absence of accident? [Text 10:6]. Insufficient similarity. [Text 6:4].
63. Relevancy, 352. [Text 10:6, 6:4].
75. Relevancy, 352. To show motive. [Text 10:7].
77. Relevancy, 352. Admissible under *Castro*? Crime involves false statements. [Text 15:7].

79. Can Don assert privilege not to testify against spouse? Note date of marriage. [Text 33:10].
83. Relevancy, 352. Is this "collateral" impeachment? [Text 15:3, 32:15].

G. People v. Howard Dowling

4. Hearsay. Overruled: 1250 State of Mind Exception (but not to show Howard's conduct.) [Text 23:4]. To show effect on listener? (Why she read diary). [Text 19:4]. 352. Relevance—Her state of mind not in issue.
8. Relevance/352. Sustained: Strike "Because I was worried about things she told me re: Howard" [Text 2:1].
10. Hearsay. Overruled: Admission by conduct. [Text 19:5].
12. Hearsay. Threats by Howard—Included in 1370? [Text 27:6]. Secondary Evidence—Contents of Diary; CEC 1523—Original lost. [Text 31:2].
14. Relevance. Overruled: Admissible to show bias. [Text 15:4]. Secondary Evidence: Contents of Will? [Text 31:2]. Improper opinion as to value of property. See CEC 813. [Text 29:3].
26. Hearsay, irrelevant. Overruled: Bias, but telling mother irrelevant. [Text 2:1].
28. Irrelevant. Sustained: Bad character; 352. CEC 1108. Exception inapplicable. [Text 11:1]. 31.1. Privilege. Overruled: Defendant has standing under CEC 918, but 972 (f) only applies if husband arrested or charged before marriage. [Text 33:10]. Can privilege be asserted to former testimony? Privilege did not exist at time of testimony, thus not waived. CEC 1291(b)(2).
2. Instruction to jury—violate 913? [Text 33:8].
3. Hearsay. Declarant unavailable? Is refusal "infirmity" if not based on fear? [Text 25:3].
4. Prior testimony?—Cannot be offered by prosecutor; No opportunity to cross. (1291). [Text 26:2].
32. Hearsay. Overruled: State of mind exception. [Text 23:4].
40. Hearsay. Overruled: To show effect on listener (Howard knew). [Text 19:4].
42. Hearsay. Overruled: Admission by Howard. [Text 20:1].
52. Hearsay. Overruled: Not admission: offered by defendant. [Text 20:1]. Spontaneous/ Contemporaneous 1240/41. [Text 23:1].
55. Hearsay. Sustained: Not admission; Not admissible because not offered against defendant. [Text: 20:1].
57. Non-responsive, irrelevant traits of character. [Text 12:1].
58. Improper character evidence. Overruled: Ok under Michelson cross-examination of opinion witness. [Text 12:1].

60. Irrelevant. Bad character. Misdemeanor may be admissible under Prop. 8 if shows dishonesty. [Text 15:7].
66. Irrelevant. Overruled: Refusal to speak shows bias. [Text 15:4].
76. Improper opinion—beyond expertise. [Text 29:6].
80. Improper opinion—beyond expertise; argumentative. [Text 32:11].
86. Secondary Evidence—oral description of contents. [Text 31:2].

H. Paula Pringle v. Thomas & Neeley

3. Hearsay. Overruled: Not admission (offered by her); Non-hearsay purpose: to prove knowledge. (Limiting instruction should be requested). [Text 19:4].
7. Hearsay. Overruled: Authorized/Adoptive Admission. [Text 20:4]. Declaration Against Interest? (Declarant unavailable). [Text 25:6].
9. Hearsay. To prove knowledge? Show effect on listener. (Limiting instruction). [Text 19:4]. 11. Polygraph results. CEC 351.1 applies only to criminal cases. Irrelevant. *Kelly-Frye* test should be applied. [Text 29:4]. Hearsay, Secondary Evidence, Authentication. [Text 21:2].
14. [Q by Plaintiff!] Reputation. Hearsay declarant? (Not admitted for hearsay purpose). Effect on listener. Note reputation exception CEC 1324. Bad reputation of witness is admissible, but she hasn't testified yet. [Text 15:1]. Bad Character—Propensity; CEC 1106 shield applies. [Text 15:1]. [Move to strike].
15. Hearsay. To show knowledge of listener? [Text 19:4].
18. Hearsay (what secretary saw); Spontaneous statement? [Text 23:1].
19. Opinion—rationally based on perception? [Text 29:1].
21. Hearsay. Statement of intent? [Text 23:5]. Dying declaration? [Text 25:5]. Secondary Evidence [oral testimony]. [Text 21:2].
25. Relevance? Admission of Neeley's note makes him a hearsay declarant, so his character can be challenged under CEC 1202. [Text 15:10]. But no bad character evidence offered. [Text 15:2]. Beyond scope of direct. [Text 32:12].
27. Irrelevant, bad character evidence to show disposition; 352. [Text 11:3]. Double Hearsay. What secretary said may be admitted to show knowledge of listener. [Text 19:3]. What Floyd said secretary said could come in as admission under CEC 1224. [Text 20:4].
29. Bad character. Question Ok under *Michelson*, but this is civil case. [He testified to good reputation on cross]. [Text 12:1].
31. Hearsay. Overruled: To show effect listener & state of mind. [Text 19:4].

34. Lack of authentication. [Text 30:1]. Secondary evidence. [Text 31:2].
36. Hearsay. Authorized / Adoptive Admission? CEC 1224. [Text 20:4]. Declaration Against Interest. [Text 25:6].
38. Bad Character re other girls. 352. [Text 11:3]. Hearsay? Non assertive. [Text 19:5].
40. Hearsay. Sustained. Bad character. May come within 1101(b) exceptio. No belief of consent is limited to prosecutions, but may show plan; intent. [Text 11:3].
41. Bad character. Opinion re: honesty admissible to impeach. [CEC 786]. [Text 15:1].
43. Hearsay. Overruled: No assertion.
47. Relevance? To show bias, interest or motive. [Text 15:4]. Hearsay? To show effect on her mental state. [Text 19:4].
51. Hearsay. Overruled: Admission. [Text 20:1]. Relevance. Overruled: To show bias, interest. [Text 15:4].
56. Relevance. Deacon in Methodist Church (Note CEC789)
58. *Kelly-Frve*. Accepted in "Scientific" community? [Text 29:4].
62. Hearsay. Normally relied upon by experts? Not admissible for truth. Highly prejudicial, 352. [Text 29:5].
71. Rule of Completeness — CEC 356. [Text 20:1].
77. Feeley polygraph — Waive *Kelly-Frye* objection by eliciting this? [Text 32:4].
80. Improper opinion. Beyond expertise. [Text 29:6].
82. Privilege? Relevance. Lack of bias? [Text 7:2].
85. Improper bad character evidence. Specific acts not admissible in civil cases. [CEC 787]. [Text 15:3].

J. Pearl Price v. Ford Motor Co.

1. Hearsay. Overruled: Statement of intent to prove or explain acts or conduct. [Text 23:4].
3. Hearsay (2) Pearl: Non hearsay purpose — to show effect on listener. [Text 19:4]. John: Statement of intent exception. [Text 23:4].
5. Relevance. Character Evidence. Excluded by CEC 1104 — character with respect to care or skill. [Text 10:6]. (Tactics — may prefer to rebut this with bad character evidence, rather than object and exclude). [Text 32:13].
7. Same. Admissible as evidence of habit? [Text 14:4].
9. Hearsay. Overruled: Statement of Intent. [Text 23:4]. Non-hearsay purpose to show condition? [Cf. lines 29–36 *infra*.] [Text 19:4]. Authentication of phone call.

11. Prior accidents. Excluded by CEC 1104. [Text 10:6]. Opened door by "good driver" testimony? (if admitted). 352.
20. Improper character evidence. Prior conviction of reckless driving. To impeach hearsay declarant? [Text 15:10]. Admissible under *Beagle?* [Text 15:6]. Not relevant to credibility; 352 prejudice. "Plea bargain" inadmissible. [Text 9:1].
23. Insurance. Relevance? (Offset Damages?) CEC 1155 inapplicable—not to show negligence. [Text 8:2].
29. Improper opinion. Overruled: Rationally based on perception. [Text 29:1].
33. Hearsay. Overruled: Prior inconsistency? Not inconsistent? [Text 21:1]. Party Admission under CEC 1224/1227? [Text 20:4].
35. Hearsay. Lack of complaint non-assertive. [Text 19:5]. If hearsay, admissible as admission under CEC 1224/1227. [Text 20:4].
46. Hearsay. Not admission (offered by plaintiff). Dying declaration? Not under sense of death. [Text 25:5]. Spontaneous? (1240–41) [Text 23:1].
48. Opinion. Qualified as expert? Need not be if rationally based on perception. [Text 29:1].
50. Opinion. This would require qualification as expert. [Text 29:3].
52. Hearsay. Spontaneous? (1240–41) (12 minute lapse). [Text 23:1]. Report (Four objections): (1). Hearsay: Bus. Record? CEC 1271. [Text 24:2]. (2). Blood alcohol results—bus. duty to report; Secondary Evidence. [Text 31:5]. (3). Mrs. Worth Hearsay. No business duty to report. [Text 24:2]. Inconsistent? No. Spontaneous? (4). Improper Opinion re: drunk/asleep. [Text 29:1].
60. Opinion—qualified as expert. [Text 29:3].
64. Other accidents. Relevance. Knowledge/ Notice to Mfr? No showing of similar circumstances. [Text 6:4]. Hearsay/ No Personal knowledge. [Text 18:3].
66. Recall—Subsequent remedial measures. Admissible where strict liability alleged. [Text 6:1].
68. Personal knowledge? [Text 18:3]. Beyond expertise. Relevance—punitive damages. [Text 2:1]. 352.
79. Relevance. To show bias. [Text 15:4].
81. Relevance. To show bias. Amount paid is admissible under CEC 722. [Text 15:4].
87. Hearsay? Not to prove truth, but state of mind of declarant. [Text 19:4].
92. Hearsay? Prior inconsistent statement. [Text 21:1]. Entire report?
99. Relevance? To show bias? [Text 2:1]. 352.

K. People v. Peter Scott

3. Lack of authentication of phone call. Hearsay. Non-hearsay purpose (establish time of death). [Text 19:4]. Statement of intent. [Text 23:5].
5. Hearsay. Statement of intent. [Text 23:5].
7. Not hearsay: Silence not intended as assertion. [Text 19:5].
10. Hearsay. Overruled: Admission. [Text 20:1]. Irrelevant. ("I was surprised"). Opinion? Speculation. [Text 29:1].
12. Opinion, No personal knowledge. Sustained: Strike "a month before he killed her." [Text 18:3]. Hearsay. Sustained: Exception in CEC 1170 would not apply. [Text 27:6]. Irrelevant, improper bad character evidence. Overruled: CEC 1109 exception would apply. [Text 11:4]. 352 Overruled.
15. Hearsay. Prior Inconsistency. [Text 21:1].
18. Hearsay (Newspaper article). Objection by examiner. To show effect on listener. [Text 19:4]. 352. Opened door on cross examination. [Text 32:3].
23. Improper character evidence. Sustained: CEC 1102 only allows good opinion in rebuttal. [Text 10:4].
24. Irrelevant, improper character evidence. Sustained. Not within CEC 1109. [Text 11:4].
27. Improper opinion. [Text 29:1].
29. Irrelevant. Impeachment by prior conviction. Not a felony, but Prop. 8 may allow if moral turpitude. 352. [Text 15:7].
31. Irrelevant, hearsay. Both overruled: Relevant to show bias, [Text 15:4], hearsay exception for state of mind of declarant. [Text 19:4].
33. Hearsay. Prior Inconsistency. [Text 21:1]. Motion to strike opinion re "looney" granted.
37. Irrelevant, re "dating." Overruled: Shows motive. [Text 2:2].
39. Irrelevant re "married." Overruled: Shows motive. [Text 2:2]. Hearsay. Admission exception. [Text 20:1].
41. Same.
43. Irrelevant. Overruled: Comes within CEC 1109 as domestic violence. 352 overruled; admissible to show propensity. [Text 11:4].
48. Hearsay. Overruled: Admission exception. [Text 20:1].
49. Irrelevant, improper bad character evidence. Sustained: Does not relate to honesty. [Text 15:1].
55. Irrelevant. Overruled: Shows possible bias. [Text 15:4].
57. Irrelevant. Sustained: Arrests, not convictions; not related to honesty. [Text 15:1].

65. Hearsay. Overruled: Shows state of mind of declarant. [Text 19:4]. Relevant to show bias or interest. [Text 15:4].
70. Improper opinion. Sustained: Beyond expertise, not qualified re: condition of bodies. [Text 29:3].
75. Irrelevant. Must show similar conditions. [Text 6:4].
77. Irrelevant. Overruled: Admissible to show bias. See CEC 722. [Text 29:8].
83. Hearsay. Sustained: Cross of expert using book which is not conceded to be authoritative. See CEC 721(b). [Text 29:7].
85. Irrelevant. Improper character evidence? Overruled: Goes to qualifications, not character. [Text 29:3].
96. Improper opinion, speculation re: Mrs. Neeley. Sustained. [Text 29:1].
97. Hearsay, secondary evidence. Sustained: Where is the receipt? [Text 31:2].
99. Opinion re: honesty admissible to attack character of witness. [Text 15:1]. But other statements stricken: No specific instances permitted; opinions must relate to character trait of honesty. [Text 15:3]. 352.
103. Irrelevant. Overruled: Admissible to show motive. Prohibition of evidence re: insurance inapplicable. [Text 8:4].
114. Hearsay. Overruled: Prior inconsistency [Text 21:1] and Party Admission [Text 20:1].
115. Irrelevant, improper bad character evidence. 352. Close question, may go to motive. [Text 2:2].
117. Irrelevant, improper bad character evidence. 352. Sustained: Does not come within "domestic violence" exception of CEC 1109. [Text 11:4].
119. Same.

L. People v. Don Defiler

2. Improper conclusion or opinion: I was "raped" and "sodomized." Must elicit factual details. [Text 29.6].
4. Hearsay. Overruled: State of mind of declarant, effect on listener. Would also come within exceptions for contemporaneous statement or excited utterance. [Text 23:1].
6. Hearsay. Overruled: Party Admission. [Text 20:1].
8. Hearsay. Overruled: State of mind of declarant, [Text 19:4], or statement of future intent. [Text 23:4].
10. Hearsay. Overruled: Party Admission. [Text 20:1]. Offer to compromise? Is CEC 1152 limited to civil cases? Would it be abrogated by Prop. 8? [Text 7:5].
15. Irrelevant. Sustained: Excluded by rape shield law. [Text 13:1].

18. Hearsay. Overruled: Statement of intent exception. [Text 23:4]. Rape shield? Admissible to show defendant's reasonable belief re: consent? [Text 13:1].
20. Hearsay. Not admission, because not offered *against* defendant. [Text 20:1]. To show state of mind of declarant? [Text 19:4].
22. Hearsay. Statement "mother insisted" offered to show effect on listener. [Text 19:4].
24. Hearsay. Prior consistency? To show "fresh complaint." [Text 21:5].
26. Hearsay. Prior Inconsistency. [Text 21:1].
28. Hearsay. Prior consistency. [Text 21:5].
34. Hearsay, secondary evidence. No foundation as business record. [Text 24:1]. Where is the report? [Text 31:2].
36. Hearsay. Extrinsic proof of prior consistent statement, but not prior inconsistency. [Text 21:5]. No medical exception for hearsay. [Text 23:7]. Same conclusions as line 2, *supra*.
42. Rape shield? May come within exception: Not to show consent, but alternative source of injury. [Text 13:4].
44. Hearsay. No medical exception. [Text 23:7]. Ordinarily relied upon by experts? [Text 29:5].
50. Improper Opinion. Must *Kelly-Frye* test be met? [Text 29:2].
56. Hearsay. Sustained: Not admissible as prior consistency. [Text 21:5].
58. Hearsay. Defense may prefer not to object, but to offer rebuttal. [Text 32:13].
64. Hearsay. Cross examination with text not conceded to be authoritative. [Text 29:7].
72. Improper evidence of bad character. 352. Overruled: admissible to show propensity under CEC 1108. [Text 11:1].
78. Irrelevant. Overruled: Shows bias or interest. [Text 15:4].
84. Irrelevant. 352. Overruled: Admissible to show consent. Rape shield law does not apply because she is not the victim in case on trial. [Text 13:1]. Little risk of prejudice to parties. Invocation of privilege may be rejected, on grounds she waived privilege by testifying on direct examination. [Text 33:4].
90. Rape shield? Not to show consent, but to impeach her claim of no prior anal intercourse. [Text 13:4].
92. Irrelevant? Impeachment by contradiction; whether it is collateral would be addressed by 352 objection. [Text 34:15].
94. Hearsay. Overruled: To show effect on listener. [Text 19:4].
98. Irrelevant. Overruled: Not to show bad character, but to show consent. Rape shield law inapplicable. [Text 13:1].

100. Improper character evidence. Overruled: Opinion of bad character for honesty admissible. [**Text 15:1**].
108. Irrelevant, improper character evidence. Prop.8 might permit misdemeanor if shows moral turpitude, but 352 could exclude due to remoteness (ten years old). [**Text 15:7**].
110. Irrelevant. Sustained: has no relevance to honesty or veracity. [**Text 15:1**].

Epilogue

Evidence

(To Tune of "Camelot")
By Gerald F. Uelmen

A law was passed a distant moon ago here,
A code which doesn't make a lot of sense,
But every student of the law must know it,
    It's Evidence.

When opposing counsel puts on his Star Witness,
And judge and jury listen too intense;
It's time for lots of frivolous objections,
    From Evidence.

      Evidence, Evidence
      Sometimes it may seem like a lot,
      But in Evidence, Evidence,
      You'll learn objections on the spot.

The character of a witness can be challenged,
By conviction of a felony offense,
But not if its a minor misdemeanor,
    In Evidence.

The hearsay rule has numerous exceptions,
Including one for dying declarants,
But only if the truth is what's asserted,
    In Evidence.

> Evidence, Evidence,
> You can recite the Federal Rules,
> And in Evidence, Evidence,
> Make your opponents look like fools.

When there's danger that the truth may be exposed,
You must object on grounds of relevance,
A limiting instruction should be given,
> In Evidence.

And when you're in the courtrooms of our nation,
In the daily war for dollars and for cents,
You'll use the tricks we taught,
By clients you'll be sought,
And always you'll be grateful,
For our course in Evidence.

Index

ADMISSION, 4, 10–11, 18, 23, 26–28, 30–31, 33–34, 42, 47, 51, 56, 59, 79, 81–83, 99, 107, 109, 121, 124–125, 127–128, 209–220
   Adoptive, 82, 109, 215–216
   Authorized, 12, 82–83, 109, 209–210, 215–216
   Implied, 5, 82–83, 87, 212
AGENT, 12, 82–83, 99, 109, 210
ALIBI, 74, 81
ASSERTION, 79–80, 96, 129, 210–212, 216, 218
ATTORNEY-CLIENT PRIVILEGE, 137–139, 210
AUTHENTICATION, 121, 123, 209, 211, 215–216, 218
AUTHORITY, 14, 44, 82–83, 109, 119, 173, 209, 213
AUTOPSY, 15, 120, 171–173
BIAS, 29, 31, 56, 87, 89, 106, 120, 209, 212–220
BLOOD, 13–14, 19, 102, 145, 191, 217
BURDEN OF PROOF, 134, 143–145
BUSINESS RECORDS, 95–96, 110
CHARACTER EVIDENCE, 4, 35, 37–38, 41, 49–50, 53, 55–56, 61, 66, 118, 126–127, 209–212, 214–221, 223
CHILDREN, 8–9, 47, 69–71, 106, 118, 126, 144–145, 161, 168
   Child Abuse, 47, 62, 71, 93, 105–106, 110, 117, 126, 160
   As Witnesses, 57, 69, 99, 129

CLIENT, 128, 137–139, 197
CO-CONSPIRATOR, 83, 209
COMMON DESIGN, 42
COMPETENCY, 30, 67, 69–70, 73, 102
COMPLETENESS, 81–82, 129, 216
COMPROMISE OFFERS, 29
COMPUTER RECORDS, 96
CONDITIONAL RELEVANCE, 11–13, 46, 73, 97, 109, 121, 123
CONFESSIONS, xvii, 4, 54, 99
CONFIDENTIALITY, 5, 29–30, 134
CONFLICT OF INTEREST, 139
CONFRONTATION, RIGHT OF, 105, 127–128
CONSENT, 48, 51–52, 134, 183, 216, 220
CONSISTENCY, 87, 211, 220
CONTEMPORANEOUS STATEMENTS, 91
CONTROL GROUP, 138
CONVICTIONS, 9–10, 39, 41, 50, 55–59, 82, 96, 209, 218
CORPORATION, 99, 138
CREDIBILITY, 7, 39, 52, 55–56, 58, 66, 70, 80, 85–88, 118–119, 134, 210, 217
CRIME OR FRAUD EXCEPTION, 137
CROSS EXAMINATION, 16, 51, 70, 81–82, 118, 126–127, 151–152, 167, 183, 218, 220
CUSTOM, 53–54
DAMAGES, 8–9, 75, 147, 217
DEPOSITIONS, 101–102

INDEX

DISCLOSURE, 29, 133–134, 137–138, 204
DISCRETION, 5, 13, 15, 25, 48, 56–58, 69, 73, 89, 118–119, 126–128
DIRECT EXAMINATION, 16, 58, 62–64, 70, 119, 126–127, 151, 155, 159–160, 163–164, 167, 169, 171–172, 174–175, 177, 179–180, 183–185, 189–191, 195–199, 201–203, 205–206, 220
DIRECTED VERDICT, 143
DOMESTIC VIOLENCE, 38, 47–48, 106, 218–219
DOUBLE HEARSAY, 102, 210, 213, 215
DUE PROCESS, 4, 10, 47, 57, 74, 105, 128–129
DYING DECLARATION, 97–99, 111, 211, 213, 215, 217
ETHICAL RULES, 85
EXCITEMENT, 91–92
EXCULPATORY, 74, 81–82, 99, 102, 111
EXPERT, 13, 81, 117–120, 160, 163, 171–172, 177, 191–193, 195, 198–199, 201, 203, 209, 211–213, 217, 219
EXTRINSIC, 18, 21, 23, 27–28, 33, 55–56, 85–87, 102, 144, 220
EYE WITNESS, 117
FEDERAL COURTS, 28–29, 69, 87, 96, 120, 138
FORMER TESTIMONY, 97–98, 101–103, 214
HABIT, 53–54, 212, 216
HEARSAY, 3–5, 7, 11–13, 33, 58–59, 71, 77, 79–81, 85–86, 89–90, 92, 95–99, 102–103, 105–107, 109–112, 118–119, 121, 125–129, 134, 209–220, 223
HEARSAY EXCEPTIONS, 4–5, 12–13, 71, 77, 79, 95–98, 105, 107, 109, 112, 134, 219, 223
HOLDER, 133, 137–138
HYPOTHETICAL QUESTION, 120
HYPNOSIS, 71

IDENTITY, 6, 12, 14, 38, 42–43, 45, 95, 118, 121, 134, 211
IMPEACHMENT, 9, 57–59, 85–87, 120, 127, 210, 214, 218, 220
INCONSISTENCY, 70, 85–87, 209–211, 217–220
INSURANCE, 31, 112–113, 174, 190, 200, 217, 219
INTENTION, 92, 112, 137
JUDGES, 14, 17, 57–58, 69, 128–129
JUDICIAL NOTICE, 95, 119, 141, 147–148
JURORS, 5, 15–17, 25–26, 69
  Anonymity, 26, 52
  Deliberations, 25
  Privacy of Jurors, 25
JURY VIEW, xvi
LIMITING INSTRUCTION, xvii, 18, 79, 125
MANTRA MOTION, 127–129
MARITAL PRIVILEGES, 134
MEDIATION, 5, 29–30, 133
MEDICAL DIAGNOSIS, 93, 110, 211
MEMORY, 43–45, 70–71, 73–75, 86, 89–90, 93, 110, 211
MENTAL ILLNESSS,119
MORAL TURPITUDE, 39, 57–58, 209, 218, 221
MOTIONS, 3, 26, 125
MOTIVE, 8, 31, 38, 46, 87, 101–102, 106, 111, 212–213, 216, 218–219
NEGLIGENCE, 8, 27–28, 31, 46, 57, 118, 210, 217
NEGOTIATION, 30
NOLO CONTENDERE, 33
OBJECTIONS, xvii,101–102, 111, 125–129, 151, 155, 159, 163, 167, 171, 177, 183, 189, 195, 201, 207, 210–221, 223
OFFER OF PROOF, 52, 73, 85, 125, 144
OFFICIAL RECORDS, 95, 110
ORDER OF PROOF, 73, 118
OPINION, 9, 13, 27, 37–39, 45, 49–50, 54–55, 61–65, 70, 88, 95, 112, 117–120, 161, 164–165, 168, 172–173, 179–181, 185–187, 192,

INDEX

196, 198, 200, 204, 206, 209, 211–221
PAST RECOLLECTION, 89–90, 110
PERSONAL KNOWLEDGE, 12–13, 67, 69, 73, 98, 111, 210, 212–213, 217–218
PLEA BARGAINING, 18, 33
PREDECESSOR IN INTEREST, 102
PRESUMPTION, 26, 96, 143–145, 147
POLICE REPORTS, 95, 110
PREJUDICE, 5, 15–18, 31, 42, 47, 56–57, 126–127, 212, 217, 220
PRELIMINARY HEARING, 70, 88, 97–98, 102
PRELIMINARY QUESTIONS, 11–13
PROBABILITY, 18
PROPENSITY, 18, 38, 42, 46–47, 53, 57, 64, 66, 210–211, 215, 218, 220
PHOTOGRAPH, 15
PRIVILEGES, 4, 11, 23, 131, 133–134
  Attorney-Client, 4, 137–139, 210
  Marital, 134–135, 173, 211
PRIVITY, 102
PROBABILITY, 18–19
PROOF, xvii, 9, 11, 19, 26, 31, 42, 45, 49–50, 52–53, 73, 85, 87, 118, 125, 134, 143–145, 220
PROPOSITION EIGHT, 3, 133
PUBLIC POLICY, 18, 27, 144
QUALIFICATION, 73, 117, 217
RAPE SHIELD, 5, 51–52, 219–220
REFRESHED RECOLLECTION, 89
RELEVANCE, 1, 11–14, 42, 66, 73, 97, 102, 109, 121, 123, 129, 214–217, 221, 224

RELIABILITY, 105–107, 186
REPUTATION, 37–39, 41, 45, 49–50, 55, 61–64, 66, 165, 169, 184–185, 212–213, 215
RESIDUAL HEARSAY EXCEPTIONS, 105
SEXUAL ASSAULT, 38, 47, 51
SIMILAR ACCIDENTS, 28, 217
SIMPSON, O.J., 13, 15–16, 48, 54, 56, 81, 102, 106–107
SPONTANEOUS STATEMENTS, 91
STATE OF MIND, 80, 92–93, 209, 212–215, 217–220
SUBSEQUENT REMEDIAL MEASURES, 27–28, 217
SUCCESSOR IN INTEREST, 102
SUICIDE, 98–99, 184
SYNDROME, 117, 201, 203–204
TESTIMONIAL, 107
TEXTS, 119
TRUTHFULNESS, 55, 62–64, 66, 209, 212
ULTIMATE ISSUE, 118
UNAVAILABLE, 53, 81, 93, 97–99, 101–102, 106–107, 110, 134, 179, 214–215
VICTIM, 30–31, 38, 41, 43, 45, 47, 49–52, 70, 74, 87, 92, 106–107, 117–118, 201, 203–204, 210, 220
VOIR DIRE, 69
WAIVER, 18, 58, 102, 111, 126, 133–134
WORK PRODUCT, 133–134
WRITINGS, 12, 89, 121, 123